THROUGH THE DEPTHS
A TRUE LIFE STORY OF THE ARMENIAN GENOCIDE

by

Souren H. Hanessian

Gomidas Institute
London

Souren Hanessian memoirs have been produced here with the silent editing of spelling errors, minimal changes to the text for clarity, and corrections in the use of foreign terms. Every effort has been made to retain the original quality of the work without giving it an undue polish. The family tree was appended by Karen Cizek. We thank her and her relatives for making this work available to us for publication.

© 2017 Gomidas Institute

ISBN 978-1-909382-38-1

Gomidas Institute
42 Blythe Rd.
London W14 0HA
United Kingdom
www.gomidas.org
info@gomidas.org

Souren H. Hanessian (*l*) and his wife
Christine Miadzinian (*r*), cir. 1930

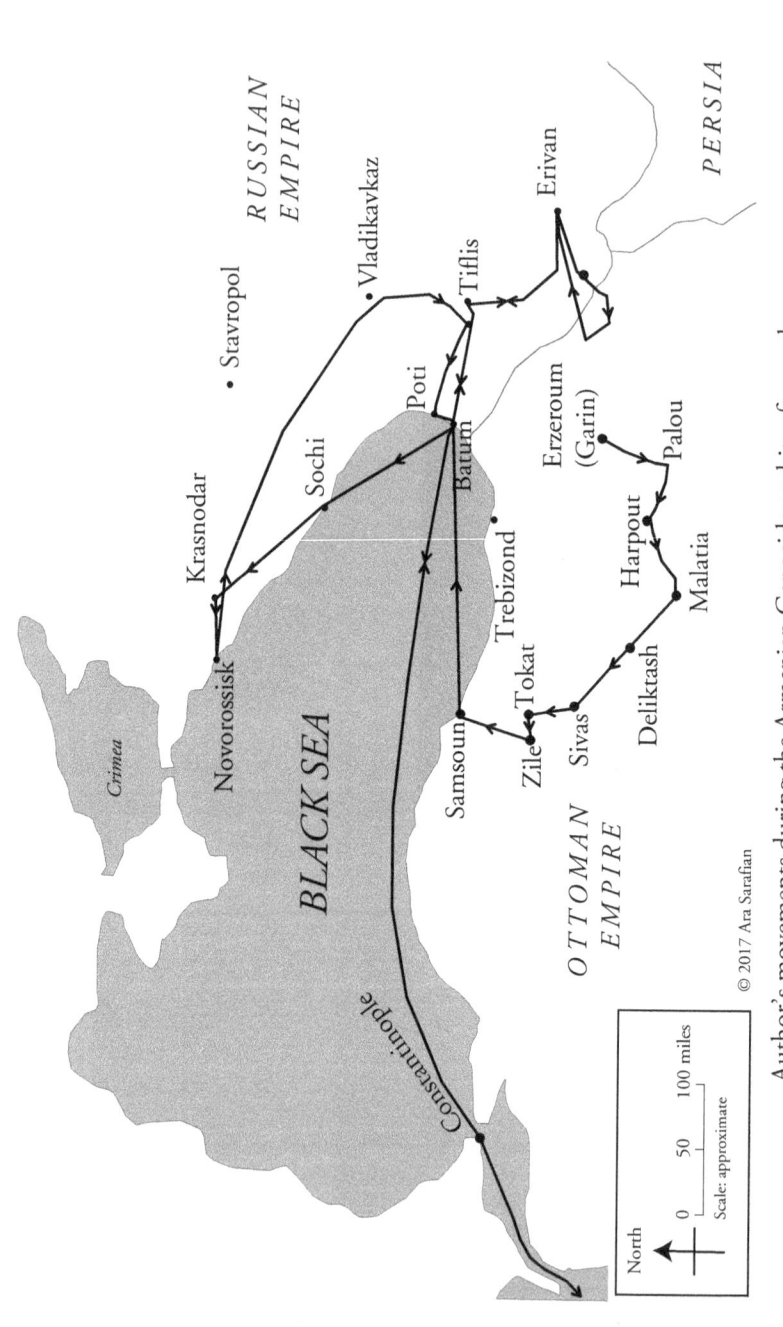

Author's movements during the Armenian Genocide and its aftermath

PREFACE

My grandfather came to the United States from Ottoman Turkey as a young man. Here he met and married a fellow Armenian Genocide survivor, Christine Miadzinian. He became Vice President of The Americanization School Association of the District of Columbia which helped immigrants newly arrived in the U.S. to adapt to their new country. He also became an attorney who specialized in immigration issues. He and my grandmother raised two sons and two daughters, including the baby of the family - my mother. They raised their children to love the United States and to appreciate this country for its unique ability to incorporate immigrants into society without destroying their culture of origin. They raised their children with an appreciation of the rich Armenian culture. They also raised them to respect and understand other cultures. In fact, my mother's childhood best friend was a Jew. As young girls their parents arranged for them to "trade places" one year at each other's religious schools. My mother spent a year in Hebrew school, and her friend spent a year in Episcopal Sunday school. Both sets of parents believed that understanding other cultures was that important.

My grandfather wrote the following memoir with the intention that his story should not be forgotten. He sought no financial gain; in fact he never attempted to have the manuscript published. He simply wanted his story, one of many such stories to come out of the Armenian Genocide, to be remembered. I wish I could say his story was unique in human history. Unfortunately, it is not. His story takes its place in history among the countless stories to come out of mankind's struggle with the plague of Genocide. In the twentieth century alone a partial list of genocides would include: The Armenians in Ottoman Turkey, 1915; Jews, and others, in Nazi Germany, 1940s; Cambodia; the Khmer Rouge, 1970s; the Kurds of Iraq, 1980s; Bosnia and Herzegovina, 1994; Rwanda, 1994.

I hope someday the government of modern Turkey will admit what happened during the Ottoman period, the way the modern German government has done regarding the Nazi era. Armenians all over the world are waiting for that admission and apology to help us heal.

Sharing this story is my way of honoring my grandparents. I hope it helps the world avoid another genocide.

As for my grandmother's experience as a young girl during the genocide, the family knows very little. In the words of one of my uncles "it was not something she spoke of."

I never got to know either of my grandparents: they died before I was born. But I did have an Armenian "grandmother." She was my grandmother's best friend and fellow genocide survivor and immigrant. During my high school years, I would visit her for a week or two each summer. I remember cooking Armenian food and talking about my own mother's childhood. (I learned a few things about my mother's teenage years that she never volunteered.) I also remember being woken several times by the sound of her screaming in her sleep. We met in the hallway and all she said was "The Turks." Like my grandmother, she did not wish to speak of it further.

Following this document are some family photographs. They are all taken in the US. No photographs from "the old country" have survived. I have also included a family tree. My uncle Jack (Sarkis) Kossayian did extensive geneology research in the late 1970s. Since this was before the internet, his research involved traveling to South America and interviewing elderly relatives to preserve their memories of the names of family members. I have added the standard symbols for gender as well as a few dates and new members of the family.

God Bless,
Karen Cizek,
Arizona
2015

THROUGH THE DEPTHS
A TRUE LIFE STORY OF THE ARMENIAN GENOCIDE

1

Until I was about eleven years old I lived a happy free life of childhood with my family in my city of Garin, which is also called Erzeroum. This is one of the ancient cities of Armenia with crooked winding streets and many stone houses. School, home and play, great interest and love for my immediate family, and deep admiration for some of my young uncles, filled my young life to the uttermost.

In the summer of 1914 my father, who was a banker, took my mother to Tiflis and I was sent on my vacation with my aunt to the Holy Cross Monastery ten miles from Garin. Perhaps the mountains of Armenia are much like mountains here, but as I look back and remember the streams and rivers, the hills and woods, each and everything clothed with its legends, there seems a great difference to me. An eight-hour trip in a cart drawn by a string of black yaks brought us to an ancient site where many people camped and spent the summer days. Nearby was a monastery where priests of the Armenian Apostolic Church, who aspired to be patriarchs of the church, hid away from the sound of living voices. Here around the cathedral during the period of the Roman Empire, King Haik built great walls twelve feet thick, so that this might be a place of shelter, sanctuary, and protection for the Armenian people.

Sloping up on one side was the mountain Mahmour-Dagh, so called because the mountain looks sleepy, dark and mysterious. On the other side were natural caves in the rocks, and if you called, your voice resounded in many echoes until you thought the mountain alive with many people. Here, too, an old legend tells us, the baby Christ was brought and was cradled in a rock. There was a stream as clear as crystal with water so pure and cold that it was a joy to drink from it.

Walking about a mile from this Cathedral you reach the Heart (Sird) River. It flows between mountains and its beautiful valley makes an ideal spot for the students from Sanssarian College of Garin. This was in Armenia and was founded by Mugerdich Sanassarian, and was given by him to the Armenian people of Garin.

The Heart River flows through the land of "The Khachapayd Vank" which means the "Monastery of the Wooden Cross" from the legend that Christ bore his cross into this land and here stopped to rest it. It is here, too, that legends recount that Saint Gregory the Illuminator, founder of the Apostolic Church, was slain by a woman and since that day no woman dares step on the holy ground within the walls, or if perchance she enters, she does not die but returns broken and crippled.

If you follow the river, you quickly reach the Aboulian Falls, where the clear, sparkling water drops a hundred feet or more and nearby is the beautiful Oughd Geyser, named so because the form of this with the land about resembles the form of a camel. Oughd Geyser is the great head and at the camel's feet are a thousand little geysers known as the Bin Geysers. In this river swims the Rajah Fish; the fish of royal color. The spawn of this fish is specially noted for its sweetness and is considered a great delicacy.

Here among the craggy hills beside the swift flowing water, the students of a few years ago were wont to pitch their tents and make their summer camp. Not far away near the village of Ozny, gardens extended where, in the summer, folks raise many vegetables. Here the students and vacationists rest and play.

One beautiful day of this eventful summer of 1914 my cousins and I went to the river to swim and fish. While we were there, a group of Turkish lads came and when they saw us they lifted their heads with an unusual show of pride. They annoyed us and tried to create a disturbance. We hurried home with a strange impression of unrest. We knew nothing definitely. We were only youths at play but the coming events had cast their shadow.

When evening came, the elders returning from the city brought stories with them of the moblization of horses and cattle. This had to be for the use of the army. Were the Turks to moblize? My aunt decided to return at once to the city and learn the truth concerning these many reported rumors.

The journey home was an anxious one, driving many miles, not knowing what the day would bring, thus making the homeward trip long and tiresome. When we reached Garin, I was greatly surprised to find my parents there. Quick to sense the unrest in the air, the Armenians from across the border hurried to their home towns. "Much can happen in a single day." They wanted to gather their dear ones together, and so my parents hurried back from Tiflis, where they were, to protect their home and children.

The feeling was about that the Russians might sweep over the country any day. The Turkish army was being mobilized, men were being drafted into service. The Great War was beginning in Europe. Would Russia and Turkey be drawn into it?

Uncertainty lasted. Days passed, no one knowing what would happen. The Turks needed money as much as they needed men and so, by paying, my uncles and father were able to stay at home and not enter Turkish army service. Not so my mother's brothers. One had just been graduated from the Harbiye Military Academy of Constantinople, another was an optician and a third a dentist. They were all pressed into the Turkish service.

Winter came at last and the city of Garin was blanketed with snow. The rough roadways were covered, sleighs dashed by, and still we waited uncertainly. Now actual trouble began. The Turkish government was seizing merchandise. My father and uncles were importers of sugar. Their factory was in Russia. They were told that their produce had to be surrendered to the government. With the aid of Armenian friends, some of the merchandise was carried to a place of safety under a church and hidden there.

Shortly after this, my mother was visiting friends. As she came home, someone called her from a passing sleigh, "Your brother has been shot!" For my family, the actual warfare had begun. My mother, always so dignified, brought up in a convent, and always careful of her demeanor, thought only of her favorite younger brother, Vahan. She fled through the snowy streets to reach him. The wound was not serious and Vahan recovered, but of that, more later. I tell this because it was the first step.

2

Two months had passed since my young uncle Vahan had been brought home. My grandmother's house was close to our home and my mother spent much time in nursing and caring for him. The elders watched for a small Turkish news sheet called "The Telegram". This brought the news from the Turkish-Russian front.

My father and mother were always strangely quiet. Young as I was, my heart was full of dark foreboding. We went about our regular duties; school life and home life were the same in appearance. Faces smiled but within, hearts were heavy.

A special church holiday was approaching and the patriarch was to preach at the church.* All of the city was preparing for this event. I was one of the choir boys.

The night just before the celebration my father came home late. His face was ashy white. I saw my mother's startled look. I listened but nothing was said. My father was silent. All through the night the sense of tragedy weighed upon me. Before light we were up and I was ready to go to the church for the early service.

I can close my eyes and live each detail of that morning now. The dimly lit church; the cold piercing air that made the blood tingle; the incense burners; the pungent odor; the priests in their rich robes; the patriarch in his vestments; the choir boys with their high young voices singing the praises of God and then, suddenly, as a swift moving cloud, several men entered the church. They were the leading merchants of the city and I knew them to be friends of my father and of my great uncle. The men hurried to the patriarch's side. My place in the choir was close to the patriarch's chair. I saw the good man's face blanch. I bent my ears to hear as the men whispered.

Suddenly I caught the name of "Pastermadjian." This was my great uncle, one of the wealthiest men of the city; the supervising director of the Imperial Ottoman Bank of Garin.†

The patriarch said a few hasty words, drew his robes around him, and without saying mass, hurried away with the men from the church. The priest continued the service. Unnoticed, I slipped in back of the other boys and hurried out by the priest's entrance. My one thought was to reach home. I rushed into the house calling my mother. Two aunts were there. Evidently they had hurriedly dressed in black. Where was my mother? My baby brother was crying. I wanted my mother. What was

---

* This "patriarch" was probably the prelate of Erzeroum, Bishop Smpad Saadetian (1871-1915)

† This was probably Setrag Pastermajian, assassinated in Erzeroum on 10 February 1915.

this awful mystery? My aunts took me with them and together we went swiftly through the snowy streets. I knew now that death had come to my uncle, but still I did not know how. We passed a corner where the snow was dyed with blood, and then went up into the upper story of my great uncle's house. This was the first time I had stood in the presence of death. I stood filled with awe and fear. A bayonet had been thrust through my uncle's temple and a knife plunged into his back.

His great fur coat bore mute testimony of how the butchers had executed their task. He only spoke two words when they found him, "My children." My aunts and mother knelt around his beloved body. In the east it is the custom that they draw their veils over their faces so others might not see them weep. My mother had not known when she left the home, so she alone was not in black but rather dressed for the church holiday. Something broke in my heart. I was no longer a youth without care. From then, my life was changed.

At about three in the afternoon the church bell began to toll. It was like the wailing of a voice, a sob that resounded in all the hearts of the town. Slowly the bearers carried the body of the man who had been their foremost citizen to the church. Slower, slower the bell tolled, until at last it ceased. The body rested here in the church.

The next day special male singers came together; the body was borne forth to be laid in its last resting place. With voices breaking with sadness, the funeral chant was sung. The body was placed on the "rest stone" and the final service was read. Then all moved forward to the crypt.

3

After the funeral of my great uncle, twenty tense days passed. My mother was almost constantly with my young uncle Vahan who was still very ill. With him she laughed and talked – the lips laughed, but the heart wept. Her eyes carried the haunted look that I now know means fear – not for oneself but for loved ones. Life again moved as it had moved before. Our daily tasks were done. The order of the home was not interrupted. The servants attended to all the small things of the house as usual. My father came and went to his business place but the cloud was drawing nearer.

No one could tell how nor when the storm would break but its approach was felt.

The small daily war sheet, "The Telegram," brought the next definite news. It announced that a well known Catholic Armenian had given up the faith of his fathers and had accepted that of the Turks. His family had adopted the Turkish customs of "drews" (Turkish veils for the face) and harem life. The Christian Armenians were greatly shocked.

This man was an able leader. He was a man who went to and fro between his own people and Turkish diplomats – a man to whom his own people had turned. Now he was no longer one of them. The holy bond of a common religion was broken.

Events followed swiftly. The dread calm of waiting was over. By next morning all Armenian guards had been ordered from the streets and in their places were Turkish policemen. Our hearts were turned to ice. Our fathers had lived through massacres before.

Was such a blow to fall upon us again? All day the Turks patrolled the streets. The diocesan bishop called his colleagues together and they all went to the governor of Garin to ask for the government's attention. As soon as they left, the Governor's messengers were sent to the leading men calling them again to a conference. I remember my father hurrying away to the meeting. Again the people waited. That evening a notice was posted on the church wall bidding "All Armenians of the city to assemble early in the morning." Late that night my father went with a few men to Turks whom they knew to be real friends. They now knew the orders which were to be made public at the church the next morning. They were told if they would change their religion all would be well. With heavy hearts the men returned.

Sleep was far from the eyes of the people of Garin on that fateful night. With the first cold streaks of dawn, family groups could be seen winding their way through the narrow streets to the church.

Mothers, fathers and little ones knelt close together to receive the bishop's blessing and then all rose to hear the message. The Turkish government ordered that for the safety of Armenians, all must leave the city. As Garin was so close to the Russian border, the Turks feared for the loyal Armenians! Hence they would be conducted under military guarantee to Ourfa; a place of safety. The Turkish government guarantee was given.

At the motion from the patriarch all knelt. I hear the chanted prayer now:

> Have mercy,
> Have mercy,
> Have mercy,
> Have mercy,
> Come Father and hear our supplication.
> Lead us in the best way.
> Before Thee do we prostrate ourselves.
> Give freedom to our people.
> Please God Please God Please God Please God.

And from the pulpit over the heads of the kneeling multitude floated the voice of the bishop:

"We pray to the Heavens that happiness and peace may be the portions of that which is to be ours."

4

Garin stands at the edge of the great plain where one branch of the Euphrates rises. The city looks out over this plain and, rising high above it, on the far side is Eyerly Dagh or Saddle Mountain, some 10,690 feet in height. Here too is Kermeth Dagh which is well fortified. Five thousand Turkish troops are quartered here, as this is a strategic point of great importance. A highway runs through, connecting the Black Sea port of Trebizon and the Persian city Tabriz. During the trading season hundreds of camel trains pass through, bearing imports and exports – hence Garin is one of the leading trade centers of Asia Minor.

In June of the year 1915, a great trading caravan bearing rice and soap was in the city from Palou. The order had now gone forth that four hundred of the leading Armenian families must leave the city by Friday morning. The destination was to be Ourfa and the reason given was the danger for Armenians if they remained so near the Russian-Turkish front. A council of leading merchants was called and it was decided by this group of men to enlist the traders with their horses to aid in the deportation.

Can you picture the life in my home during those few days? Forty-eight members of my father's family were to go. These included my father's brothers and sisters, with their wives, husbands and children. My mother's people were not ordered to depart. There was much to be done; the necessities were to be packed. Jewelry and table silver were taken to the imperial Ottoman Bank of Garin to be placed in vaults for safe keeping. Rugs of great value and special furniture were taken to the American Mission to be cared for in our absence. My brave mother worked busily carrying the heaviest burden in her heart. I went with her when she sought the advice of Mrs. Stapleton, the American missionary. She knew that within a few days the time would be fulfilled when she would give birth to another child. How should she travel over this rough and dangerous path through the mountains so that we and the little one would survive? A wagon could be procured, or should she travel in a "maffa"? A maffa is made of boxlike contrivance, one placed on each side of a horse and so balanced that the boxes hang comparatively level. It was decided that this was better than a wagon because of the rocky, rough roads and steep ascents.

Friday, the fateful day for departing, approached. Orders were issued by the local government that no arms or ammunition were to be taken. The Turkish military governor would provide a squadron of gendarmes to protect the travelers. The caravan was to be ready to pass through the city gates at ten thirty o'clock.

The sun rose clear – a perfect morning, June 16, 1915. There was no hint in nature of the travail in human hearts. Excitement was everywhere among my people. The Armenians who had been the servants of the families of wealth were at every home – tears in almost all eyes. Parting gifts of money and jewels from masters and mistresses were given to those who were to stay behind and serve them no longer. Did their hearts say that there would be no need of service? As I walked close to my mother's "maffa" and we made an ascent to the gate of the city, I turned many times and looked back at the thronged city streets; at the home of my happy childhood; saw the spire of the church where I had been one of the choir boys; the place where my great uncle lay buried. You, of the west, can you imagine that gaily colored picture and dream of the depth of sadness in our hearts? The sun is shining hotly and the many colored umbrellas are raised to shelter eyes from the glare. Feeble women, little children, great bundles of tents, mattresses and food are packed on the horses' backs. Men and women are walking, boys and girls walking and running. The drivers of the pack animals call to their horses. Smiles and tears swiftly chasing one another on many faces.

The bishop was making an effort to get certain Armenian men who were serving in the army hospital excused so that they might join their families in the flight. These were soldiers pressed into the Turkish Army but transferred to the Armenian Red Cross Hospital to aid in caring for wounded Turks. Two of my cousins were among their number and the families were sad indeed leaving the city, with these beloved ones being left behind.

At the end of an hour we had reached the city gate. Here were two tents, one on each side of the road. We realized then that the officials were going to make sure that the order "no firearms to be carried" was obeyed. Every man and woman was taken into the tents and searched. All baggage was ruthlessly searched and thrust through with sabers and spikes to see that nothing was concealed. Then we moved on. Our way led through a mountain pass like an open door.

So, we lost sight of our city. We saw only the mountains covered here and there, where the sun does not strike, with dazzling snow. And so we trudged on until three in the afternoon. Then the order was given to halt. The long line stopped. Men and women busied themselves pitching their tents, cooking the first meal, washing and resting. The animals were fed. The leading men sought the Turkish officer in charge and asked how long they judged it would take to reach the town of Ourfa, our destination. No satisfactory answer was given. Darkness came and our first night passed in peace and quiet.

The next morning at daybreak all were astir. The march began early. All day we walked on the rough roads. At three in the afternoon we rested again. The women were busy washing, and the men preparing for the night, when we were all surprised by groups of horsemen gathering a short distance across the valley. They were in sight of all and must have numbered fifty or sixty. From their dress we recognized them as soldiers known as "chettis." These men have certain privileges under Turkish rule. They go in search of deserters from the army and, generally speaking, are known for their cruelty and wildness. We were told that they were in search of deserters and that we need not fear because of them.

Our men remonstrated because our women must leave our camp at times and we greatly feared for their safety. The officer, however, sent his servant with a message to the "chettis" and about twilight they rode away. A great happiness had come to us this day. The bishop's efforts had been rewarded and about forty-five Armenian men joined the caravan. They were the soldiers who had been pressed into hospital service in Garin and were now allowed to join their families. My two cousins were among them and great was the joy of their wives and brothers because they were once more with us.

The next three days passed without startling incident, or at least none that came to my childish eyes. The journey was wearisome but no one minded. Walking from dawn until three or four o'clock is not easy for men, women and children and we were footsore and tense because of apprehension. The third night several shots were heard nearby and one old lady was killed – who knows whether by a stray bullet or with intent! We were told that the "chettis" were in the neighborhood seeking deserters.

The fifth day we came to the famous Bingel Dagh. This is the mountain range, one part of which is close to Garin. About two in the afternoon, when we were going through the mountain passes, a single "chette" approached the gendarmes' commander and gave him a message. This I now suspect was a plan by the bandits to show which way we must be led. That night there was almost continual shooting in the neighborhood and the weaponless train of travelers rested not at all.

The sixth day we came to the more open country again. The mountains slope turned abruptly into the valley. The valley was open with a small river on the far side. With the unobservant eyes of childhood, I did not realize the drama of my family. My mother rested at the side of the trail, the women gathered around. With no conveniences, with no skilled attention a baby girl was born. One hardly noticed the pause. Half an hour and we were pushing on again – another life added to the caravan. And my mother, convent-bred, whose home had always provided her every need and comfort, was pushing on with the others.

At night the shooting resumed. At daylight the gendarme commander came to the men and told them that his soldiers refused to provide protection unless they were well paid. The Armenians came together and took a collection, giving each soldier about twenty-five liras, and diamonds to the commander. Suddenly more shots began to be fired from the same hiding place.

The gendarmes had given their oath to protect us. Some of them hurried away and soon dragged back a Kurdish boy about twenty years of age. They brought him in front of the Turkish gendarme commander and demanded of him why he had fired upon a train of women and children under their protection. Two Armenians stood by who knew the Kurdish language. As the soldiers beat the boy, he called on "why lemen babo." which means "my father" to protect him. Finally he told them that the chettis had made them fire. As the boy was thus convicted, the commander drew his revolver and killed him before he could finish his statement. But now the Armenians understood the true significance of what was said: "He had been told to shoot!"

The caravan started again on its weary way. The women had not understood the full significance of what had happened. The men knew, however; and by their nervous movements and looks showed they were seeking a way of escape. We traveled on until nearly one o'clock not knowing from minute to minute what would happen. Suddenly the caravan halted. The traders whose horses were being used to carry the weak and feeble ones and the baggage demanded that all the money they were to be paid should be given to them at once or they would abandon the caravan. The men gathered together at once and paid the balance of the money owing.

An hour later we came to a small village. Here the advance guard turned off the road and followed another direction. Some of the Armenians, familiar with the road, realized that this was not the way to Ourfa. The commander of the gendarmes insisted, however, that this was a shorter way and that time and distance must be saved. When we had traveled about six or seven miles, we came to another steep incline at the foot of which was a narrow valley opposite a river: it was dark, silent and foreboding.

We passed a flour mill and all came down the incline slowly: horses, men, women and children. Now we were in the open and could see the many Kurds, some on horseback, some walking, but slowly approaching our train across the valley. A group of chettis were galloping at the base of the far mountain. We judged that they were the same ones we had seen before but they were too far away from us to clearly distinguish them.

Nearby, however, the mountainsides were full of Kurds. They came almost up to our caravan. The commander gave the order for us to push on until we should reach another village.

At a turn in the road where the river sweeps around the mountains, we came face to face with the mounted Kurds. The Turkish gendarmes passed the word that they would drive the Kurds away and then we could proceed. Some baggage was quickly taken from the horses' backs and stacked and the women and children put behind it. We could see the Kurds very near us. The traders began hurrying away with their pack horses, carrying our beds and valuable rugs. A fight began between one of the traders and a Kurd. The Kurds were attempting to take the rugs. One of my people knew all these places well. He broke through the pressing Kurds and hurried to Sheikh Koy, which was a village nearby. The village sheikh was well known to him. If he could reach Keghy [Kighi] it might be possible to get government help. Everyone would know that this was a caravan of the richest Armenians of Garin. They would profit well by saving us. Anxiously we watched for his return. At last he came bearing the message, that if we could pay 5,000 liras and jewels, he could protect us for a single day. But we must come empty handed, leaving our baggage behind us. Again the caravan started with bands of Kurds riding close on either side. Fear was in all hearts now. Our brave fathers and older brothers were helpless – not one had a weapon. The fathers carried the little children. Boys and girls bore bundles.

We came to the village of Sheikh Koy and were driven into a stable, dirty and foul from animals. The sheikh gave us his promise of protection. Our Armenian guide slipped away to try to get word to the Turkish government soldiers at Keghy.

I cannot describe that night. Men, women and children were packed into a place of unspeakable filth. My mother tried to protect the newborn babe. The Armenian priest knew in his heart what was coming, knew that death was certain and yet he encouraged us. Prayer and songs went up to an unanswering God. All night the Kurds shouted their curses, threatening that the children would be slaughtered, that the women would be raped! One's flesh quivers as the anguish of those hours is recalled.

In the early morning they opened the doors and allowed us to come out to get some bread. Wild-eyed men watched us, greedy for money and jewels which had not already fallen into their hands.

We recognized the head of our kinsman who had gone to seek protection for us hanging from a beam. His body had been slashed and hung in pieces. His wife and children became hysterical with grief. Their cries pierced the morning air.

As we stood huddled in a great crowd thinking the end had come, we heard the rapid approach of horses. Once more the chettis appeared. They carried with them a message that they were to protect us. They called to my father and two or three others and swore on the "Koran" that they were honest and this time would protect us.

Our desolated line was again ordered to march. It was impossible for my mother to walk or stand any longer. My father was allowed to buy a horse at an exorbitant rate from the Shiekh's people. We moved forward up a steep hill. This was the eighth day of walking. We were jaded, weak, weary and without sufficient food. Children cried and clung to their mothers and fathers. We, who had never known want before, faced desolation. As we reached the top of the steep hill we begged that we might rest – we were too tired to move on. But no, we could not stop. "You'll rest in the valley, but not now!" the Turkish commander told us. We moved across the crest of the hill and began the descent into the valley. Suddenly a loud whistle rang out. The gendarmes and Kurds, together, turned on our line. Shots and saber strokes rained around us! We were in the midst of HELL. One man tripped and fell as he ran down the hill and many fell over him. Of all the hundreds in the line, in a few minutes, only three boys, two men and forty girls and women were alive. We began running, not knowing whither, our clothes torn from us, with everyone wounded.

Then a gendarme with human feeling came up. He began firing on his own people. He saw the chief bandit take the most beautiful girl in the caravan. The girl's mother called to her: "Anahid! Anahid! Anahid!" But we saw that she was already dead. The kind gendarmes called us together and ordered soldiers to give us clothes. Bleeding, dazed and blinded by utter desolation, we started on again. We saw more Kurds, but nothing mattered now. Nothing worse could happen. Fear had gone out of our hearts. These Kurds from Dersim had come to truly help us. There was little left to do.

We followed the trail until it came out onto the main road, the one from which we had been detoured so that we might be cut to pieces off the highway. The Turkish post traveled on this road. For the present our little band of about forty was safe.

5

When we reached the road it was early morning. The officer with the human heart ordered the gendarmes to go to the near villages and seek asses or donkeys to aid in transportation. The section we were now in was mostly populated with "kizilbash" (red headed) Kurds. They were kind and willingly gave their animals to carry the wounded women. We were all, men, women, and children, wearing old and dirty Kurdish rags. At last our caravan started again with those who were most seriously hurt on the backs of animals.

Only the thud of our weary feet and the tramp of the asses could be heard as we moved forward. We silently made our way onward. Present sufferings and the cloud of horror that had been ours for the last few days crowded out all else. We climbed a hill and when we reached the summit we could look into the valley of the Kara Su. The quiet peacefulness of the country in the morning light surprised us. This mountain was "Gavour Dagh" [Infidel Mountain], the mountain of Christian dogs.

We walked on, probably for a mile before we came to a slow running river. There on the shore, in this peaceful spot, we saw the body of a man without clothes. He had evidently been killed for some time for the flesh was putrid and the air foul. We were so filled with our own grief and suffering that we had not dreamed there were others suffering too. We asked the drivers of the asses what it meant. They pointed to an Armenian village now nearby, toward which we were going. Heavy indeed were our hearts. Near us were some beautiful white mulberry trees. All of this belonged to Armenians. As we approached we saw many bodies under the trees.

It was about three in the afternoon now, rain had started to fall, and we had no place to go or water to drink. When we saw a spring, those who were able ran like animals, so great was their thirst. Physical suffering was crowding out all other thoughts. We starved here in the open at night. Early in the morning we slowly moved on again and a torturous movement it was. After a weary march of many miles we came to a hillside from where we could look down on the town of Palu.

The towers of the fortress rose high on the opposite bank. We saw the great bridge spanning the Eastern Euphrates River. It was one of the largest in Anatolia.

Soon we came to a spring where we halted to rest. Here we met two Armenians who were going to the gardens outside the city. They had heard of the attack on our caravan by the Kurds and "chettis." We also learned that the traders who had disappeared with the pack horses loaded with our merchandise had come this way, and that the governor of Palu had ordered the gendarmes to hold all the goods. They were now stored in the Djami (the Turkish Church [*sic*, Mosque]). We also learned that about half of the Armenian population of Palu had been deported that day and that others were to go the next day.

It was almost dark as we entered the city and we wondered what would be our fate. The gendarmes led us to an empty house near a great bridge. Guards were placed at the doors so no one could enter and also to prevent our leaving. Here we stayed for two days. Much was crowded into the long hours.

From the windows we could see the Armenians who were starting on their deportation. They looked as we had looked so short a time ago – gay in colored clothes, with many pack animals bearing their merchandise, families and relations keeping close together. We pressed our faces to the windows watching the scene before us. Across the long bridge the road climbs the mountain side covered with vineyards. As we watched from our point of vantage we could not understand the meaning of orders that had evidently been given to the gendarmes. At the long bridge the procession was being halted, the men being kept on our side and the girls and women being sent across and up the mountain. The view was sinister. What could it mean?

As night approached we huddled close together. We tried to care for one another's wounds as best we might. We had come down from the high plateau of Armenia and here at Palu the weather was warm and all the dangers of infection were ours.

The whole town was quiet from dusk to midnight. After that, strange sounds came to us. The voices of people pleading. "What is it? What is happening?" we asked one another. Anguish pressed down upon us. What was happening to those other Armenians out there at the bridge? In the morning we saw! Hundreds of men's headless bodies were out there in the Euphrates River. Around the fortress was a sunken moat. This was filled with men's and children's clothing. We saw no more and dared not ask the guards.

During the morning hours the "kaimakam" (mayor) of Palu came to make inquiries concerning the attack on our people. He knew many of the Garin people. Special inquiries were made for the Pastermadjian family and we were asked if any were in the group. He told us how his officers had saved our merchandise from the traders who were making off with it and that it was safe in the Djami store-room. He ordered the police to choose one of each family and conduct them to the store-room so that they might identify their own possessions. My own aunt and my father's sister-in-law went with the police. Shortly afterwards they returned with a number of bundles and packs. It was good to get many necessary things; bedding, underwear, linen to bind up the wounds and supplies so that we could better care for our sick.

It was only the third day since we had come to this town, and our condition was pitiable indeed. Some of those that were suffering the most lost their minds and raved in delirium. A young girl lost her speech. One, who was a distant relative of my own family, saw something belonging to her when the merchandise was brought in. With a laugh of a maniac, she sprang upon it and slashed it with a knife; there were her jewels hidden away. Horror had followed horror so rapidly that our minds were benumbed.

We were told by the governor that we must push on to Harpout. He could not find transportation for any but the most helpless, and he had no way to forward our belongings. However, he told us we would have the privilege of auctioning our goods. I can remember some of my family's heirlooms that we had brought with us, Russian blankets, rich rugs and bales of the finest kid. We decided to try to keep the kid. The other things were sold for practically nothing.

That night, as we planned for our departure, smoke strangely filled the city. We learned that the clothes in the moat of the fortress were being burned. What else we did not know.

The order came again for us to leave early the next morning. The men and boys had to stay, the order said. When we entered Palu, we had all been covered with Kurdish rags and the men and women could not be distinguished. Now again the two men and two boys in our group were disguised with women's clothes and veils. I was one of these.

At last we were ready and emerged from the prison house where we had been for three days. As we crossed the bridge where the dread tragedy had occurred two nights before, we met some women with six small children. They had come from Keghi. We suddenly recognized one of these women as my teacher to whom I had first gone to school. She had spent part of each year in Garin and then, when the school closed, went home to her family and parents. When she saw and recognized us she began crying afresh and her swollen eyes and sad look told of her sorrow before her lips moved. She told us of her husband's death. She too was ready to die. Many of the women were also ready to die. They were fighting with their hearts. In their hearts they were praying to God to let them die. They could endure no more.

On we went up the rocky mountain road, for that way lay our journey. High on the mountain lay a great rock, over which the road wound. The road was covered with gravel and dust. As we drew near the rock my teacher stooped down and gathered a handful of gravel and dust. Suddenly, before we could stop her, she thrust the dust into her mouth and gathering her two children within her arms, jumped from the high rock down, down to the bed of the Euphrates River. The gendarmes were anxious for they had been ordered not to lose the women. There was no use lingering, however, as she was already dead. We could do no more for her and she could suffer no more at the hand of the Turks.

For two days we travelled in our small caravan. Only those who were wholly unfit were on the asses' backs. We had little to eat and drink. Death would have been a relief.

We came, after two days, to a small Armenian village, or rather a town where the Armenians had their own churches but followed many Turkish customs. Here we were given our freedom by the gendarmes and allowed to stay if we wished. But our people felt that they must go on to Harpout.

That was a city where there were other nationalities. We felt that we could have our sick cared for there. We dared not tell our news to the Armenians whom we met else we would be killed. Some of us went to a spring and there we met some Armenian women. We tried to tell of the massacre but they would not believe us. We stayed that night in the village and were treated kindly. In the morning we felt stronger for the day's journey.

After five hours travel we arrived at the town of Husseinig. We found many Armenians assembled here. They too had received orders from the Turkish Government to leave. We cautioned them as to what they might expect, but they were sure that no harm would befall them as it had us, as they were to have the protection of the Turkish gendarmes.

A civilian approached our group of people and told us that orders had come for us to go to a school near Harpout.

We traveled on without any notable incident past the main city near the Armenian cemetery. Here the school we were seeking was located. As we drew near we saw tents pitched around the cemetery. We were surprised to find many people from the villages round our city Garin. Tired and ill, we felt that we had reached our journey's end.

American missionaries came to us. They were not allowed to ask us questions. They offered us clothes, but since we had recovered our baggage in Palu, we did not need them. As I remember, it was interesting to hear Americans try to speak Armenian. The missionaries asked the governor of Harpout if our sick and wounded could be put in hospitals and gained his consent. For that night I stayed at the National Turkish School.

6

This was Harpout, the city where we were to be protected. Of all the hundreds of us that had left Garin less than thirty entered Harpout. Among these few were my mother and my uncle's wife. Both were sent to the hospital with almost all the others. I was to stay at the school.

The next day I was looking out the window wondering what was best for me to do. I was only a lad of twelve. I laugh now as I think of my making decisions about so momentous a question which undoubtedly involved life and death. As I watched from the window, there was a crowd, and I soon saw that they were villagers from my old town. These people had been traveling for about two months. They looked jaded and worn, with rags for clothing. I decided that it was better for me to get away from the school if I could and go to the hospital. But there seemed to be no way to escape. Several hours later as I watched the people outside, I saw a man who had been a tenant on my father's farm outside of Garin. I attracted his attention. He grew greatly excited upon seeing me. After we talked furtively for a while he found a rope. He tossed the end of the rope to me and I climbed out of the window, letting myself down by the rope which I fastened to furniture inside the room. I stayed with these people five or six hours and then I ran away, my idea being to reach the hospital and be with my own people again.

When I reached the hospital I saw my uncle's wife. She was a woman of great beauty. In Garin she was considered one of the most beautiful of all women.

It was decided to keep me in the hospital and let me work in the pharmacy. One of my uncles was a pharmacist and I had often been in his store in Garin. So a new life began for me.

7

Red Crescent Hospital. Several days after this, the deportation started from Harpout again. After three large groups had been sent from the city, news came back to us that all were being killed instead of being sent on the other places.

Throughout the city the policemen searched to find Armenian politicians and priests. The town criers went about saying that the Armenians were to leave the city. They announced that if a Turk tried to protect or hide an Armenian, he would be hung before his own house. Horrible things were happening. Priests were brought to the hospital every day to be treated; they had been tortured to compel them to tell the secrets of the Armenians. Often their feet and bodies had been burned. Their persecutors did not want to kill them. The information they were supposed to have made it wise to keep them alive. Death would often have been easier than suffering.

The Red Crescent Hospital, for such was the name, was situated between the two cities of Harpout and Mezere. Around it was a garden which was a public garden (millet bakjassy). Here coffee and drinks were served and often there was music and dancing. It was a place of happiness and pleasure.

One afternoon about three o'clock word came to the Hospital that it would be searched. The principal of this institution was a good man, one who had done much to bring comfort to us. Now he bade some young Armenians to run up into the attic to hide. There was a tiny room up under the roof; he told me to go there. I hurried to the room. I was excited and frightened. There was a small window and I could see into the garden. There was a wild group of men entering. I knew they would get the Armenian girls.

The door of the little room suddenly opened and my aunt, my beautiful aunt, entered. She ran crying to me; "Souren! Souren! Souren!" She was covered in blood from a number of wounds where she had been stabbed. I opened the window and looked out. The wild drunken men were driving a group of Armenian girls before them. They were forcing them to dance using awful threats. Their clothes were being torn from them. The girls were crying. The men broke branches from the trees and beat the girls with them. I cannot tell the awfulness of it. One poor girl was tied to a tree, a girl, a Christian girl, was covered with oil and set on fire. Where was the Christ? I turned back to my aunt. There was nothing I could do. The death agony was on her face. They had tried to force themselves on my aunt. I heard the sound I knew meant death. There, alone with me, she died. She had been the pride of Garin womanhood.

8

Sometime after this the superintendent of the hospital decided to adopt me. My mother was to pay him a certain sum for each day I was to work in his store. His wife was a Greek. She had been a dancer and was greatly loved and a favorite of the Turkish officials of the city. Their son was foolish. From this time I spent almost my whole time in the store. The deportation had stopped previous to this. One afternoon I had closed the store and was going home when I saw some policemen talking to a group of Christians. These Christians were not only Armenians, but were of many nationalities. They called me and told me to follow them. I knew the officer personally and I asked them what was going to happen. They said that nothing would happen; not to be frightened; they were only going to ask a few questions. I knew this policeman liked me and felt safe. They took us to the police station. There was a garden with a high wall behind the Turkish government building. Sentries guarded the gates. When I went in I saw men of many nationalities. They kept us there for two hours; some men wept. I did not weep, but I grew nervous feeling great dread of that which was before me. Finally an order came; all Christians other than the Gregorians (the Armenian followers of St. Gregory) were to be freed. The Syrians, Greeks, all Catholics who declared they were not Gregorians were given liberty. There were twenty of us who were of the Gregorian faith. I was proud of that; I was a Christian and Gregorian. I was the smallest boy in the group that was kept in the prison. One other boy from the hospital was there. I met Armenian politicians in the jail. Some were from Constantinople. They began talking to us and asking questions.

One of these men from Constantinople, I discovered, was a brother of my cousin's wife. I had never seen him before, but we found we were of the same family. The Armenians plotted to burn down the jail and escape. Now I was frightened.

Hidden in my clothes under my arm I carried some poison. I thought I should take this rather than be slain.

About-three o'clock in the afternoon an order had been brought that we were to be marched outside the prison gates. We did not realize what was going to happen. We thought perhaps there was to be some special examination. We were marched up a narrow street, or alley. Here a squad of gendarmes forced us to hold out our hands. With long ropes they bound us together. We started moving through the main streets of Mezre towards Yegheki. This is a settlement of Armenian bread makers. The village was located on a hill two or three miles away from Mezre. We went through the village and about two miles beyond. After ascending a steep hill about a quarter of a mile further on, we saw a group of tents. The number of civilians stood about and among them stood Harpout's police commissioner. He was a fat man, but cruel looking. The civilians were armed. All carried guns and knives in their belts. All looked fierce. Here we were halted and, still tied together, were made to sit at the side of the road. There were more than fifty of us. We could sense what was about to happen to us. Then the civilians and police commissioner began talking. The officer wanted to bet how many could be killed with one cartridge. The cruel, horrible slaughter began at the far end of the line. They shot and used knives, too. My flesh crept, as I knew this was coming to me too. When they were about half through the awful task they paused. The time had arrived for them to eat and drink. Not even killing of Christians turned them from their supper.

The Armenians, tied together, shook as they looked at their dead comrades, and knew what our fate would be in all too short a time. I remember one man who had been with me in the drug store in Harpout. He sat with blanched face and trembling limbs. I thought of the poison hidden under my arm. Just then my cousin whispered to me, and I cautiously moved my hands and reached into his pocket. There was a knife which had in some way been overlooked when we were searched. He was about to cry out. I told him to be quiet and cut the rope. By the time we had finished we saw guards coming out of the tents. I can't tell how it happened. I do not remember, but suddenly I was running – my cousin was running behind me. The gendarmes shouted "adam gachdy" (men are running away). They started firing. We could hear the noise of the bullets. We were jumping and running, not knowing where – the thorns sticking in our feet. I do not know how long I ran. It seemed hours, but after a time the fear that a knife would be plunged into my back or a bullet would fell me passed away. After a time Hagop my cousin came close to me. He was familiar with the neighbourhood and he said we must go the American Missionary summer camp. The camps were on a hill. We cautiously approached; hope was alive again. We trusted we would be given protection. As we approached the camps some Armenian orphans were walking about there. We told them of our need and great was our disappointment when they said the orders were that no men could be protected there without the head missionary being notified. One of the boys came near us and said that we had better not try to see any one and try to get away the best way we could. We could say nothing in objection because we knew the missionaries were ordered to do this by the Harpout Government. As we were turning away, I remembered that I had heard that one of our servants, "Barsegh," who had been with us in Garin, was here as a cook. I asked the boy where this man could be found. He went to look for the man, who in a few minutes came running to me.

Nothing was too good for him to do for me. He took us to his room and hid us under the bed. He kept us hidden for two days, until some way could be found to send us away. The servant went to Harpout. On the way he was taken by the gendarmes, but when they learned that he belonged to the orphanage, they released him. He sought my aunt, who with my mother, was distressed because "Souren has disappeared." Destiny had directed me and once again I was with my dear mother.

9

Dramatic changes happened every day to the little remnant of my family which was still trying to cling together. It had become known that my mother belonged to the Pastermadjian family, and to protect herself, she had become a tailor in a Turkish Government official's family. A little cousin had died, and my aunt's heart was heavy because of this last loss.

The general condition in the city was once again quiet – we received money from a branch of the Garin Bank. We felt now that perhaps we could live in peace and quiet.

It was about this time a doctor who was formerly in Garin, the doctor who reached my great uncle first when he was murdered, came to Harpout. It seemed strange to see him now in Turkish uniform. His family was one of great wealth. He was to see old friends and brought interesting news. He told of an uncle of mine who lived in Sivas and was an officer in the same Turkish regiment as him. We could not believe that one of the Pastermadjian family lived.

After several days had passed, an officer from the war department came to see us seeking information. He brought news also, telling us that my "Uncle Vahan" was an officer in the Nineteenth Regiment which was stationed, at that time, in Sivas.

To all of us this news was interesting and exciting, but because of our lack of confidence in the Turkish Government, we feared that this might be a trick. My mother and aunts decided to send me to the higher official with this officer in order that I might get the news more directly. There I was shown a telegram which read, "Please send my sister and children to me and furnish necessary transportation and orderlies."

Still I was in doubt as to the truthfulness of the telegram but did not wish to show this. I assured the official that I would see him again in a few days. He showed eagerness to render service to the family of an officer.

I returned to my mother and aunts and told them of the telegram and of the official's interest, but we were still undecided.

However, a few days later, a letter written by my uncle himself was received. In this he referred to the telegram. He also advised us that another family was to accompany us. This was the family composed of his mother, wife and two nieces of an Armenian pharmacist of the 19th regiment.

10

After a conference with this Armenian family our plans were formulated. They had not suffered as we had by having been deported and hence did not suspect orders that came from Turkish officials as we did. The quartermaster in Harpout furnished a two-horse wagon and two orderlies for each family. Early one morning we left the city of Harpout, which had been our home for nine months, and started on our journey to Sivas, a distance of only about one hundred and fifty miles, but a long distance to be covered in a wagon over rough roads.

After six hours of steady travel, we reached a mountain valley near the mountain known as "Kemour Dagh" or "Coal Mountain." On one side of this mountain we saw the river Euphrates in the distance. My mother knew that hundreds of Armenian lives had been lost in this river and the beloved bodies of these victims carried away by its waters. She dreaded approaching it but at this time nothing was visible of the terrible tragedies except pieces of clothing here and there.

Before crossing this river, we had to show our certificates to prove that we were families of officers in the Turkish army in order that we might enter the city of Malatia, a town about twenty-five miles distant from this point. After the inspection at the border, we crossed the river in a ferry boat. To me this was an interesting moment for it was the first time in my life that I had crossed a body of water.

We decided not to enter Malatia until the following morning. Nearby, in the outskirts of this city, was one of the oldest Armenian monasteries. We were deeply interested when we saw its red walls in the distance, but could not show our interest because the guards accompanying us thought we were Turks. We had been told that this monastery had been kept in good condition but as we approached we found the windows broken, the cupola and cross wrecked, and evidence of animals having been kept in it for a long time. My mother feared that I would betray our faith by my expression but she did not need to fear. I had long since learned to be an actor and hide emotion. My face was trained to smile, even as the heart wept. The orderlies openly rejoiced that this ancient home of the Christian faith was despoiled, and my Mother wanted me to rejoice with them.

We spent the night at an inn in a small village known as Kemourli Keoy (Coal Village). Here there were no Armenians.

In the morning we started again, this time for about four hours before reaching Malatia, the latter part of the time going through beautiful vineyards. One incident of the morning ride stands out in my many memories. We passed a crossroad about which I inquired and I was told it was the road which let to Arabkir.

A flood of childhood memories arose. This was my father's birthplace and my grandmother's. I asked many questions but tried not to show how much I wished that our route might lead that way; how deeply I wished to see the place where my father had spent his childhood and about which he and my grandmother had told me much when I was a little child. My people had gone from there to Garin.

But we went on and eventually reached Malatia.

11

We had heard that many Armenians deported from Garin had been kept in Malatia and that some of the Armenian girls had been forced to marry Turks. I was anxious to get this information to my mother. I wanted to learn all I could of the condition of the Armenians in this city.

After a night at the hotel, I was sent to inquire about our transportation for the next stage of our journey, as the orderlies who had brought us this far were to leave us here. I was told by the commandant at the town hall that we would not be able to get transportation for ten days.

Just as I was leaving the town hall, I noticed a man working in a little store making a die. I went closer and his face was pleasant and a look of kindness was in his eyes. My heart throbbed and the warm blood surged through my veins. I had the feeling of meeting someone from home. But I feared to speak for fear it would cause him trouble. Suddenly I thought of humming an Armenian song. He could not bear to see me standing there and asked me to come in, and then asked me about my troubles. I still was not sure but I risked telling him I was an Armenian and that I was going to see my uncle. He did not believe me; undoubtedly he thought I was sent to spy. He was frightened and said some unpleasant things about Armenians. But still I felt sure my heart had not misled me and that he was an Armenian acting the part of a Turk.

I hurried back to the inn feeling sure there were Armenians in this town if we could find them. In front of the inn was an open market place. I was sent to get some fresh baked bread. As I was waiting I saw a young boy, several years younger than myself, probably about nine or ten. His face was familiar to me and I felt sure that at some time I had known him. When I went back with the bread I told my mother that I was sure there were Armenians here whom we knew about, but she wanted me to be careful and not try to discover anything about Armenians.

The next day I went back to the bakery and waited for almost three hours with the hope of seeing the little boy again. At last I saw him dressed in short pants and a blue navy blouse and carried a stick in his hand. He spoke clearly in Turkish and I could notice nothing that would confirm my belief that he was Armenian. I followed him from the bread shop for several blocks and stopped and asked him whether he could recognize me. He acted strangely but did not reply. I dropped back but kept following him. He entered a hospital or institution. A crescent over the door proclaimed the fact that it was Turkish. I went in and as I entered I heard my beloved language. It was a joy to me to hear it again but I was still anxious to know who the boy was whom I felt I knew.

A moment later my suspense ended for Mrs. Sarafian, the wife of Roupen Sarafian, a merchant of Garin, came out of one room. She was dressed all in black and seemed proud of her position in the institution. The boy was her son and went to the same school I did but was younger than I. I went to her and asked her who the boy was. She answered sarcastically, asking me why I wanted to know. Then she said he was her son. Then she gave closer attention to me as we conversed, and suddenly she kissed me and the tears could not be withheld. She recognized me as one of the children from her old home, the place of peace and happiness. "Where was my mother?" "How had our family fared?" Questions came quickly and information too. Here in this city, she told me, was one of the beautiful girls of Garin, a cousin of my aunts, married to a common soldier, living in squalor. I hurried back to my mother telling her of my discovery and of the sad news. She was shocked to hear of the girl, but scolded me too, because of my curiosity which might cost us our lives.

That night one of our orderlies discovered from my poor pronunciation of Turkish that I was Armenian. But he reassured me, telling me he was a friend, a "Kizilbash" (meaning a "red head"). I knew that these people were always kind to the Armenians. He said it was a pleasure for him to serve an Armenian rather than a Turkish family. We became very friendly with this orderly and trusted him.

I told him of my desire to see the Armenian girl who was married to a Turkish soldier and he promised me he would help me.

I was well dressed as fitted a nephew of an army officer and the orderly acted like a military servant to me even though I was only a boy.

We approached the place where the orderly had learned the beautiful girl lived. Here on the street leaning against the wall we saw a dirty soldier. My orderly told me to give an order and he would salute and obey me so that the soldier would fear me as a Turkish officer. Our scheme worked well. I asked him if he knew anyone in this neighborhood married to a "gavour" (the family of a dog [*sic*, infidel, unbeliever]). He seemed very proud in telling me that he was. When he went into the yard that the wall surrounded, we saw a woman step out of a small house. She hastily covered her face as she saw me and hurried indoors. I wanted to talk with her and my orderly again helped me. He asked the dirty soldier to help him get some grapes from the neighborhood. By asking this he managed to get the man to go with him for a few minutes and so I had a chance to see the family of Dourbak. Dourbak was so stupid that he understood nothing of my plans and went with my orderly.

I knocked at the door and spoke in Armenian. The family within were frightened but finally the boy came out, he called my name and then I went in. They cried and begged me to take them away from this awful place. Of course I had no authority to do this. I sympathized with them and I saw "Siranoush" the once beautiful girl – God alone knew of the sacrifice she had made for the sake of her mother and brother. She was so changed that I could no longer recognize her as the girl who was once the beauty of my town. She was dressed in rags. Her eyes were sad, deeply sad and told the story of her sacrifice for the sake of the lives of her dear ones, her mother and brother. She had given herself to this low Turk. I knew it was sad and I could see no future. Every moment my hatred of the Turks grew; but it was no use, I could do nothing.

My mind went to the past and I remembered the father of this once beautiful girl. He had been a revolutionist, a man who gave his life to save many Christian Armenians who were suffering under the Turkish regime. I wished he could have raised his head and have seen his wife and his once beautiful daughter. I wish I could paint the picture clearly – it is hard for me to describe the detail.

I saw the manager of the inn where we stayed and asked him whether he could find transportation for us. He said if we could get ready within an hour he could put us on the cart that carried the mail from Malatia to Sivas. This was the fastest way of traveling in Turkey. There were four cars, each drawn by six horses, that were to leave at about three o'clock. We gladly made haste and left with the post caravan.

12

All but one of the orderlies assigned to us deserted shortly after we left Malatia. The journey was difficult because of sickness at many places and we traveled in various ways in order to avoid vaccination, knowing the unsanitary condition of the Turkish medical service. Our first stopping place was Hassan Challabi. Afterwards we went on until we reached "Hassan Badrig."

I had heard this name but I did not know in what connection. So I listened as the drivers talked, and I caught from the conversation that the "Gavours" (families of dogs) were massacred in this valley. They were talking and were happy. When we came to the bottom of the hill there was a little bridge. My mother and our friends were in the first cart, I in the last one with two drivers and our orderly. When we crossed the bridge the driver noticed that one of the horses was scared. We drove on, making a sharp turn from which we could see under the bridge which we had just crossed. We clearly noticed two girls hiding. They were almost naked. The drivers decided to drive their horses up the hill and there left them by a little spring. Our orderly tried to stop these men, but they hurried back down to the bridge. The girls looked from the distance to be young, about sixteen or seventeen. When they reached the bridge I could hear the girls screaming! After half an hour the drivers came back. We moved forward to the next stop known as Dalikdash, (a hole in a stone).

This was a military post for sick soldiers. There was a little hospital there and I saw girls dressed in white nurses' uniforms. Our stay here was to be about six hours. Our orderly was trying to make me forget the horrid incident that had happened on the way, trying to make believe that those were Turkish farm girls under the bridge, but I knew better, and my heart ached within me. We had to stay in this town six hours.

While we stayed there I went with our orderly to the market place to buy bread. For me it was strange to see a woman dressed in a blue jacket and with a hat on her head. I was curious. I wondered who she could be. When we came back from the market I found out from some people that morning there were eighty Armenian girls from the American Missionary School who had beendeported, and that this woman whom I saw was an American in charge of missionary work in Sivas and who was now ordered to return there.[*] This was the only information I could pick up. Now I knew that the two girls whom we saw on the road were unfortunate Armenian girls. Six hours went quickly.

Sivas was not far from this town and the drivers made an effort to get us up there before daybreak. When we reached the muddy outskirts we knew that we had to go some distance further in order to reach the city. We did not know whether we should go first to the barracks and verify the information as to my uncle being there or not. We decided to stay in a Turkish home for the next day.

My mother and the woman who was travelling with us went out to see if they could find out about an American missionary living in Sivas. When they were making inquiries about the missionary my mother discovered our aunt and her family. We quickly collected our bags and went to stay

---

* Miss Mary Graffam.

with her. This family had left Garin when they had closed the Sanassarian College and they had accepted a position in the Sivas College.

When we went into my aunt's house, a priest greeted us. This seemed very strange to me to see and realize how the Turks had protected this priest when they had dealt with our "cries and fainting."

We were anxious to know about my uncle, and we learned that he had been sent away with the regiment to the city of Zila [Zilé].

Zila was situated to the northeast of Sivas and was considered one of the Moslem centers of Anatolia. We wondered how our people could live in that town. We were sure no Armenians were living there.

About noon-time of that day someone knocked at my aunt's door. Ever ready, ever smiling and ever willing, this was Miss Graffam, this was the woman whom I had seen the day before in the village of Delikdash. She was all excited and worried and nervous in her movements. We were introduced to her and she seemed most pleased to see us. She wanted my mother to tell her the story of the deportation, but I knew my mother wanted to forget. It was hard for my mother to remember the details of the tragic events which had befallen us any longer.

Miss Graffam, deeply interested in our welfare, suggested that she would see the Commander of the Regiment and get a pass for my uncle so that he could come to us and take us with him. She was willing to do anything and ready to supply us with everything we were in need of. She had heard much about our family. She also knew of my uncle who was a member of the Turkish parliament before the world war,[*] and who was a leader among the Armenians in their struggle for freedom and justice. Miss Graffam knew that this uncle had organized Armenian volunteers and was fighting for the Armenian people. She knew how he was working for an independent Armenian nation where the Armenians could worship in their own way and not live in constant fear of deportation and massacres by the Turks and Kurds.

---

[*] Karekin Pastermadjian (Armen Garo) was a member of the Armenian Revolutionary Federation. After the Ottoman Constitutional Revolution (1908), he was elected to the Ottoman Parliament. In 1914, before the Young Turks entered WWI, he went to Russia, and a few months later, he joined Armenian volunteers fighting against the Ottoman Empire. After WWI, he was appointed as Armenia's ambassador to the United States.

13

Two days had passed since our arrival in Sivas, and on the afternoon of the third day my young uncle, who was about twenty-eight years old, a good looking, strong young man, walked in. We hardly recognized him, although only sixteen months had passed since we had seen him. His very face and sad expression seemed changed. You could notice the hurt look in his eyes. Again, he received crying greetings. It is hard for me to picture that moment, my mother's and my uncle's meeting. My uncle was in Turkish uniform and his name had been changed to "Vahab." This was close to his name Vahan. It was not hard for us to know the reason this was necessary.

There followed a conference. He told me that I must change my name, also my mother's must be changed. We had a funny time trying to find Turkish names, synonyms to our Armenian names. They called me "Soureia" which was very close to my Armenian name. This was done for the sake of our lives and our uncle's life. Can you imagine the priest sitting on the table and trying to assist in finding Turkish names for each of us?

The following day my uncle furnished us with transportation and we started our journey to Zila. It was decided that we should go by way of Tokat where my uncle's cousin and his family were located. This cousin was a doctor in the Turkish Military Hospital. This was an interesting journey. We were happier because we were under the protection of my uncle, and it was one of the well disciplined regiments in the Turkish Army.

So with many interesting incidents we came to the city of Tokat. The greetings here were as they had been in Sivas. It was good to see relatives again. They decided to keep us there a few days and for my uncle to go forward to his regiment.

After a week in Tokat we went to Zila. This town, I should judge, had a population of about six thousand; the majority of the men were members of the Haliffa. My uncle had found quarters for us while we were at Tokat. That first night, when we reached Zila, all the Armenian officers came to see us, but they came very late after dark. We knew they did not want anyone to know of their visiting a family. My mother had to live on the top floor, and she could not go out nor see anyone according to the Turkish custom. Every day brought dramatic changes into our home.

My uncle did not want me to idle, or play in the streets, so he decided to put me in a Turkish school. Another Armenian boy using a Turkish name, who was the son of a doctor, was in this school too. The first day, dressed as a Turkish boy, I went into the class. They had a lesson in reading from the Koran. I had never seen this book before. Although I could read and write Turkish a little, the teacher in charge called me to the principal's office and I was asked why I could not read. I did not know what to answer him. At once he knew I was an Armenian. He was nevertheless very willing to give me private lessons and try and make me a Turk. The students of that school prayed about five times a day, and according to the Koran they had to wash their feet and arms five times a day. This was a lot of fun to me the first day. When we went into the school djami (Turkish church [mosque]) the Molla (Turkish priest) started the service and I had to watch the boy next to me carefully to see how he worshipped and to imitate him immediately. I wanted to talk to the doctor's son, but he was a very wise and smart boy and did not want to bother with me. So I continued in this school for five months and graduated with good marks. The reason probably for this was that I had taken mathematics, physics, geometry and French when I was younger, and these students were taking only the first year of these subjects.

I was too young to know all the cares and worries of my elders, but every evening all the Armenians used to gather together in the home and think and discuss "some way out of Turkey." We heard that the Russians had started Bolshevism, and that the Armenian people of Eastern Russia [*sic*, Armenia] had established a small republic, although the Turkish Army was advancing into Russian territory. This news came through the Turkish newspapers. We knew everything was exaggerated, nevertheless, we wanted to run away from Zila in order to go to Armenia.

The days went by quickly. Every day we heard reports that the Turkish Army was advancing rapidly into Russian territory. One day my uncle came home with the news that his regiment was to be sent to Samson [Samsoun], and that this regiment was to be kept far from the front as it was specially organized for the training of soldiers before they go into war.

It is customary in the Turkish Army when an officer is sent away from his post for the quartermaster to furnish transportation for his family, but a day later a telegram from the military commander arrived saying that "the families of Armenian officers should remain in Zila and be kept in safety." This order did not mention the families of Turkish officers who were preparing to leave with the regiment.

So that night the Armenian officers who had families came together. I remember they held a little meeting in the back of a Turkish pharmacy, so no one would be suspicious of the gathering. There were only four families who wanted to go with their husbands and brother. However, as permission could not be gained at that time from the military commander, my uncle decided that all of us should remain in Zila, and that after he reached Samson he would endeavor to get permission for our transportation.

The day arrived for my uncle to go forward and my mother wanted me to accompany him. My uncle, however, was an officer who would not act without the approval of his commander, hence would not allow this.

14

Three days later I left my mother at Zila and followed the Army.

I left a note saying I was disgusted with living as a Turk and going to the "Djami" six times a day, and that I wanted to get nearer the Black Sea in order that I might have a chance to get near Russia. I knew that my mother did not want me to be away, but I also knew she had confidence in me and would think I could reach either Constantinople or Russia.

I had saved a little money as I had been working part of the time in a Turkish pharmacy. So I took with me about twenty-five piasters, about one dollar in American money. I knew that one piaster a day would keep one alive because the days were summer days and fruit was on the trees. I estimated it would take me about ten days to reach Samson. So I started.

I had been tramping about four or five hours from Zila when I met an old man who told me it would be dangerous for me to go through a valley I was approaching as numbers of Turkish soldiers who had deserted the Army had formed a band and were fighting in the villages.

Being a youth, I did not heed his advice and went on. I soon saw a caravan of horses, cows and sheep going over the mountain and the bandits and villagers were firing on one another. They were coming rapidly in my direction. I was sure this would be the last of me. I ran back, hunting for some place to hide, but could find no place until I came to a tree on the road. I climbed this and waited there until these wild men went by. I stayed near my hiding place all night and decided to travel only in the early mornings and late in the evenings, feeling I would be safer doing this. I also was thinking that, by the time I reached a village or town, the stores would be closed and it would be impossible for me to buy anything. I was tired and exhausted from my long tramp but slept the sleep of youth.

The following day I reached the city of Amasia. I had heard that many Armenian bread makers had been kept there during the deportation and many had been forced to change their religion. A person who accepts the Turkish religion not only changes his faith, but he also changes his nationality and is known as a Turk. So when I reached this town I looked for bread makers who would have the appearance of Armenians. I wanted to ask them to tell me the best and shortest way to Samson. I did not dare to chance asking anyone and I hesitated as they could speak Turkish very well. I finally decided to imitate a poor boy and beg. I asked at a match store, and here the proprietor told me if I needed money I could sell matches and cigarettes on the streets and he would pay me. This man wanted to know where I was from and all about me, but I evaded answering. For five days I worked selling matches and saved about seven piasters – the nights I passed in the warehouse (called Han). I was sure if I stayed there for any length of time it would be found out that I was an Armenian and that I would lose my life in some tragic way, I did not know how.

One night, as I came to the Han, I saw some shipments – trains of pack horses – from Samson. The horses I learned were to start back in the morning. I bargained with one of the Turks in charge of the convoy of horses and tried to get him to carry me with him. I promised to give him twenty piasters after we reached Samson. I was willing to do anything in the way of work in keeping the horses in line. Finally, he accepted my offer, and the next day we went on.

I should judge there were about sixty horses and seven drivers. I was handling ten horses, riding the first and leading nine after me. These people generally traveled using short cuts over the mountains, so we were far away from towns and villages. It was hot summer weather, and I had only a piece of bread for my lunch each day. In this area you could not get cold water to drink as all the springs ran hot and the water had to be cooled before drinking. It was my wish to reach my uncle so that I could save my own life and try and get my mother, as I knew it was dangerous for her to remain unprotected at Zila. It was hard for me to travel for four days like this, but hope was ahead. I could see the beautiful Black Sea in the far distance on the day before we were to reach Samson. One of the drivers kept watching me, and in some way detected that I was a Christian. I was surprised when the drivers gathered around me and insisted that I pay them twenty-five piasters. I had kept the money inside my coat cuff but they insisted on having it and brutally beat me. I had to surrender everything, even the suit of clothes I wore. Indeed, I was fortunate not to have been killed.

They left me without money or clothes, but I felt sure I could reach some house because I knew we were now nearing the city and that there were many Greeks in that area. I wandered on toward a nearby village and recognized a Greek woman by her costume. I told the people of this house all about my plight. They were kind and furnished me with clothes and put me on the right road to Samson.

When I reached there I saw beautiful houses, gardens and clean streets. Somehow I knew I was not in a Turkish city anymore; the feeling came to me indirectly. It made a deep impression on me.

15

I walked on toward the business section of the town, and to my joy recognized some soldiers from the nineteenth regiment. They greeted me and took me to their top sergeant. They were all surprised and fitted me up in a small soldier's uniform and presented me to my uncle.

He laughed when he saw me, and I knew he was happy to see me there with him, but I also knew his mind was hastily traveling and he was thinking about his sister, my mother. We knew tricks – we knew they were going to harm my mother, but on account of our lives we had to act as if we were happy.

My uncle told me that they had orders to go to Batoum and they were waiting for the German ship to arrive.

That night, when my uncle was away with a few of his officer friends, the top sergeant, the clerk and my uncle's private orderly decided to hold a surprise party. So they told me to stay around. The room they occupied was opposite the "Djami" on top of a stable, and the regiment was occupying the Djami. When it was seven o'clock I saw four women in Turkish dress and with their faces covered with masks. I went up to the room and saw a table placed on the floor with many kinds of drinks and food. Soon the four girls walked in. They were all dressed in black satin and were acting in a manner that seemed to me silly. I couldn't imagine how they were expecting me to be among them, because I was just a youngster compared to the rest of the people. One of the women was a young girl with black eyes. She walked over to me and asked me if I would like to be one of the party. She also told me they had brought her specially for me. This seemed strange to me. After we sat a few minutes, one of the men rose from his chair and proposed a toast to the Turkish Army advancing into Russia. This was the first time that I had ever taken a drink. It shook me up like broken glass going through my body. Then the girls began dancing, singing and playing their castanets. More drinks and more were passed, and the middle of the night the party broke up leaving me in the room with the young girl. I knew I was acting foolish that night, but I could not remember everything. I woke up at about ten the next morning, feeling very bad for all the things that had happened the night before. Suddenly I thought of the advice my mother had given me when she had wanted me to go with my uncle with the regiment. "Please be careful, Souren, because you are only a girl [sic] to me." I thought about this and the troubled past all day long.

It was three in the afternoon when a German Manchor steamship anchored about fifty feet from the pier. The orders were given that the 19th Regiment was to be aboard before seven o'clock. Everybody rushed. I hardly knew what I was doing all that time – my mind was dazed. When the first soldiers went aboard the ship, I went with them and they gave us a first class compartment. That night I felt desperately ill. Now I knew why mother tried to give me advice and I had not obeyed. I knew if my uncle found out he would be angry and scold me. I went to the boys who had given me the party and they told me I would have to wait until we reached the city of Batoum and see a doctor.

That afternoon, about five o'clock, we saw a beautiful spire shining in the far distance, so we knew that in about an hour we would reach Batoum. When we arrived at the pier, it was getting dark. The street looked clean in the shining electric lights. This was the first time I had seen electric lights. That night we stayed on the ship.

In the early morning we went to the barracks about a mile beyond the city. We had to go through the city. It was very interesting for me to see the Russian people dressed in their bright costumes and to hear them speak Russian. I could catch a few words now and then.

As soon as we were settled, I went to a doctor and soon was well again.

16

Every day I walked around Batoum for hours - Batoum, a city of many nationalities. The climate is very warm, with much rainfall and extremely changeable. It is sub-tropical in appearance, magnolias, lemons, oranges and palms growing in the open. I was constantly trying to see if I could get more information concerning the Armenian people. We were there about two weeks when one day, one of the Armenian officers from our regiment came in with a happy face and called my uncle. He told him that Armenian representatives and representatives from different smaller republics were in town for a peace conference with the Turkish government.

This was most thrilling to us. We knew in some way we were going to get away to go to Armenia.

The Armenian officers of the 19th regiment came together and I was stationed as sentinel. Two other Armenian boys were walking around the building. I was to be notified in case there was any appearance of Turkish officers who seemed to suspect anything. In turn, I was to notify the Armenians so they might escape. I knew they held this meeting in a dark room and were very quiet.

The next day I met one of the officers in town. I was anxious to know all about the meeting, but they did not want to tell me. They probably thought I would let the secret slip out. However, I watched this officer's movements. He went to the bank and I followed him. On the second floor, we met a well dressed man. He and the officer began speaking in Armenian. They called me and I was introduced as Armen Garos's cousin (Dr. Garekin Pastermadjian). The man was very happy to meet me and told me that my aunts had escaped from Harpout and were now living in different parts of Russia. They also told me that one of the members of our family, whom we thought had been killed, was living in Tiflis with my aunt. So new hope began in me for Tiflis was not far from Batoum. Finally I consulted my uncle and he told me: "No slips" for it might cost the lives of those who were to stay there. He also told me that they were then working to get permission for my mother and the rest of the Armenian families left behind to leave Zila. So I had to live every day with the new hope that soon I would reach my aunts and "the one" who was a mystery.

During these days the political situation changed with great rapidity. We had heard that Constantinople, the capital of Turkey, was occupied by International forces. We were expecting too that they might come to our boundary line.

A day or two after this, one of the officers from the regiment told me that he would open a store for me. He would furnish everything and I could sell very cheap. We rented a store place in the "Nouria" bazaar. I was to start selling things at very reasonable prices. Soon the place was equipped and I felt myself a man, the proprietor of a store in the bazaar. I saw that I was not liked. All the tradesmen round about thought I was a Turk, and that my place was being sponsored by a Turkish officer. A few days later I heard two men talking in the place next to mine in Armenian. I called to them and they were surprised when I began talking to them in Armenian. They were happy all afternoon and showed they were glad I was there. They went out and brought in almost all of the store keepers of the bazaar and introduced me to them. My business practically doubled from that day. It was the beginning of a successful business venture. That night the new found friends invited me to dinner with them. I accepted, and as is customary, we drank Vodka.

When I opened the store the next morning my uncle walked in and showed me a telegram. It announced that my mother had arrived in Samson and was waiting for a ship that would bring her to Batoum.

Everything seemed good in my heart, my mother was coming! Someone was living in Tiflis whom we had thought dead; who it was, still remained a mystery. I had a business and the people about me knew I was an Armenian and they were my friends. Life looked bright for the first time in two years.

17

A few days later the stores were closed as the news swept through the city that the British destroyers were advancing toward Batoum.

Excitement ran high. We hurried to the beautiful tropical park located on the shores of the Black Sea and there we could see six great steamers advancing in the distance. The International armies were in Constantinople, the straits had been opened and once again our little corner was to have contact with the rest of the world. Three of the great warships came within the breakwater of the harbor, the other three stood by. The city was wild with excitement that night.

Turkish troops were being hastily withdrawn from the Russian frontier. Soldiers had been marching through the town for several days, peace was coming to the world and we were part of it.

A few days later and my mother arrived. At about the same time the order came that the 19th regiment was to go to Sivas. Many British soldiers and sailors were now in Batoum and there were crowds on the streets and at the station. Finally, the night came when the Turkish troops were to be withdrawn. The nineteen Armenian officers left the city quietly. They went to a little town of Chakova, only a few miles from this city, a town known for the production of tangerines and tea and waited there.

That night the 19th Regiment left the city. This was farewell to the Turks and our hearts beat free and our thoughts turned to a home once more undisturbed by fear and treachery. In the meantime we had rented a house and my mother was once again making a home for the fragments of the family left to her.

When the Turkish army had withdrawn, Batoum was in the hands of the International Powers. The Armenian officers who had escaped to Chakova and had been in hiding came back. A few of them joined a police force that was organized by the British commander of this Division for the purpose of protecting the lives and property of the Christians.

The days went by quickly. We were still waiting for news from Tiflis about the member of our family whom we had thought killed. Hope was in my heart. My mother heard that it was my father!

At last the day actually arrived for opening this section for trains. So Tiflis, "the beautiful city", was the capital of the Georgian Republic and was about two hundred and fifty miles away, but the border of the Georgian Republic was very close to the city of Batoum.

I remember when the first train arrived. My mother and I were anxiously waiting to see any Armenian immigrant from our city in order to get the correct information about my father whom we had heard was alive and had escaped from Dersim during the massacre. We scanned every face as the crowds poured from the train. The train was packed with Christian Georgians and Russians. These were chiefly people who had fled from Batoum with the coming of the Turkish Army. They knew all about the Turks and mistrusted this advance.

We waited there for almost three hours, but we did not see anyone whom we knew, or anyone who could give us information.

When we returned to our house we found a note someone had left for us. The note told my mother that "your sister and your daughter will arrive tomorrow." This information was not clear to us. I remember that night. My mother cried all night long as she waited impatiently for the coming of dawn. What did it mean? These years of stress and trouble, of fear and evasion, of mourning for a dear husband and father. Would the morrow give him back from the grave – who was the daughter the letter spoke of? Was it the sister believed killed in the massacre or the baby born during the deportation? Frantically she tried to unravel these mysteries.

The next morning I went to my store, and before seven my mother went to the station. It was a small passenger station, not far from us. I remember that day, when I went home at noon, my mother was still away and I distinctly remember how angry I felt because there was no food for me. It was twelve o'clock when I heard horses trotting and a carriage stopping right in front of our residence. Our home was at the corner of two streets and doors opening on both. When I left by one door I saw a very little girl walking in at the other. I did not know who she was. I rushed back into the house and greeted my aunt, asking her about my father. Although her eyes told me she was very happy, she could say nothing at first. I remember I jumped into the carriage and drove back to the station for my mother who had been waiting since early morning. During these days she was suffering, waiting for expected news to arrive.

She was totally exhausted. I did not know what to tell her when I arrived at the station but that moment went quickly. Now I can only remember that as we reached the steps of our home my mother fainted.

18

After my mother had revived my aunt began telling us the strangest story of the innocent little girl who came to my mother with the words "Mama mama."

My aunt told us news of the Armenian situation in Garin. We had not heard this from an eye witness and hung eagerly on her words. When she had fled from Harpout following the deportation, she had finally made her way back to Garin. There Armenian cavalrymen had announced that if any Armenian child found after the last Armenian deportation in the mountains of either Turkey or in Kurdish areas were brought into Garin, a reward of five liras would be given. My aunt was in charge of this work. One afternoon a Kurdish woman brought this little child to her, and told the story of how they found this baby lying by the roadside one day after the massacre of the Armenians from Garin. She told of certain particulars and identifications marks. My aunt had been with my mother at the time of child birth a few days before the massacre and had carefully noted the infant as she was wrapped up and the journey hurriedly resumed. The woman gave the dates and place. Suddenly conviction and belief were confirmed in my aunt's mind and the blood grew hot in her veins as she pressed this little one to her and thought of my father, her brother, lost in that hideous Turkish massacre. She was sure that this was his child and she took her for her own till such time as she might be able to give her back to her own mother. She was my sister!

My aunt also brought other news. She had been told my mother and I had been massacred on the way to Sivas. She was able to unravel the rumor that had awakened hope in us of my father being alive. She told us that the Armenian Committee in Garin had made an offer to every Kurd from Dersim that they would be well paid if they brought Armenians from Turkey. This Committee was headed by Prof. Roston [Rosdom] who was the principal of the Sanassarian College in Garin. My aunts were then in Harpout and this man had written them a letter in the name of my father so that they would have confidence and escape to Dersim, and then be taken to Garin. This brought to us deep sorrow and disappointment. My father was not alive.

I distinctly remember it was the day following my aunt's arrival that I began feeling chilly and ill in the afternoon. I closed my shop and went home where I found my mother also ill. I went to bed with shivering and fever. I did not know at that time that Batoum's sub-tropical climate is unhealthy for people from the high table-lands of Armenia, and that malaria was a common disease. I was a victim of this devastating disease for almost three years, never knowing when an acute attack would incapacitate me. My temperature would frequently mount with great rapidity.

19

At this time my uncle and the other officers were contemplating a return to Armenia. Financially they were in a straightened condition. Reparation [sic, repatriation] in our homeland was now the great need but means to carry this out was lacking. Batoum was now crowded – refugees returning from east to west, from north to south, resumption of transportation on the Black Sea and the expected arrival of steamers that were entering from the Mediterranean Sea would make this a business center. The Armenian officers undertook to organize a corporation and open a hotel. They contributed a thousand rubles each and elected their own officers. This was to be a community home as well as a hotel.

I too was eager to make money quickly. A few days later a ship arrived from Novorossiysk, Russia, bringing people of many nationalities, among them Armenians who were coming to Batoum to buy merchandise. To my great happiness I found friends of my fathers who had been in Caucasia since the beginning of the World War between Russia and Turkey. They had known me when I was a youngster in Garin. Frequently they had given me mettaliks [pennies] and had been in our home many times. I now invited them to our house. They told us how eager the people of Russia were to buy luxuries which had been denied them during the years of the war. They suggested that if I could return with them and take with me chocolates or sweets I could sell them for a good price. So, I decided to close my shop and undertake this trip. My mother was opposed because she knew I was suffering with fever. But I was anxious to make money – the economic need was great.

I found out that the British soldiers had a canteen and they were buying and selling things cheaply. It took me four days and about three thousand rubles to get my two suitcases packed with chocolates and a few extra clothes in a little bag. I was ready for my adventure into the newly created Russia. The Armenian friends, one of whom was a doctor and the other a mechanic, had invested nine thousand rubles in socks. From the business point of view it was not a good venture. Their advice to me was better. We were under the impression that we would be back in less than ten days and I assured my darling mother that my illness would do me little damage in that time.

The trip on the Black Sea was rough. We stopped near Sochi, a small port. Here small boats put out and crowded around us eager to buy from the merchants on board. We were advised to hold our goods until we reached the city of Novorossiysk. I was eagerly watching as we approached this port. The mountains coming near the shore and the great cliffs make this one of the most beautiful trips but the beauty did not appeal to me, young and ill and anxious to make money that would assist us in our return to our home. I noted it, but did not feel the beauty. Finally we approached the bay of the same name as the city – Novorossiysk Bay. This is more than three miles broad at its entrance. A great mole has been built inside it which creates an artificial harbor and protects the shipping from the mountain winds that rush down from the Caucasus Mountains.

A new difficulty confronted us. The new government was placing a heavy duty on merchandise being brought in and I feared I would not have money enough and that my goods would be taken. One of my friends advised me and pointed out a short, stout man who had come along side our boat in a small motor boat. I spoke to him and he told me to hand out my suitcases to him. He was paying money to the custom house so he could smuggle in merchandise. This was a new thing for me and I was too greatly afraid of this type of operation to do it.

That night when we all finally arrived at one of the hotels of this town the doctor and mechanic met me and told me they had paid two thousand rubles to get their goods passed. That was the cost of graft as it had cost me only fifty rubles to bring mine in. These friends were interesting to me. The doctor was good natured and kind, the mechanic a shrewd dealer who was constantly trying to cheat the doctor and get his stock of socks from him. He finally succeeded.

Novorossiysk is a port, but the city where we wished to sell our stock of merchandise is Ekaterinodar which, since the Revolution of Russia is known as Krasnodar. This city is about seventy-five or eighty miles inland from the Black Sea, and is on the railway line to Rostov-on-Don. It also has a number of technical schools and experimental fruit farms. I believe its population must have been about one hundred thousand. That night I went on with another Armenian friend whom we had met, leaving the doctor and mechanic at the port.

20

It was early morning when we reached the station at Ekaterinodar. The station is some distance from the city itself, but my friend decided we should walk and find our Armenian coffee shop. I was tired carrying my heavy suitcase when we finally reached the coffee shop, but fatigue soon vanished when I met a number of Armenians who knew my family and were pleased to see me. With their assistance, I soon sold my entire stock of chocolates and made, I judge, about fifteen thousand rubles. My friend, however, who had neckties to sell, wanted to find the best customers and sell for higher prices, took longer. I waited for him about a week, busying myself by going all about the town getting prices from different merchants on socks.

After a week's visit, we went back to Novorossiysk. When we reached there, there was a strange feeling in the air. Many Russian soldiers were on the street dressed in their white (cherkesski) Cossack uniform, short black fur caps and yellow boots. They were walking the streets in fours, picking up boys who were under military age. We learned from a news sheet published by the Doublavorski army that the Bolsheviks had surrounded the city of Sevastapol. All vessels had been ordered to aid the immigrants who were escaping from the Red Army. Hence we found we could not get transportation to Batoum.

We finally determined that we would travel by train to Vladikavkaz, which was on the border between Russia and Georgia, and this would cost us more than three times the amount for a steamship ticket. My friends were crestfallen and worried as they had only made a profit of two thousand rubles and did not have enough money for this trip. We arranged it, as I was able to loan them a thousand rubles apiece. We bought our tickets for four hundred and fifty rubles and left the city that night going in the direction of Georgia, but not knowing the condition of the country through which we must pass.

The Russian trains are painted red, green and blue. The red ones belong to the government. During those days, there were only red trains on this division. We were assigned to a compartment and started our night journey. At about eleven o'clock the train stopped, and as is customary at every station, hot water being sold to travelers for making tea. Being among the youngest, I ran out to get our pot of hot water. I went first to the wash room and then ran for the hot water and jumped onto the train as it started. I looked for my friends but could not find them. I went all through the train, I did not see the faces I had seen before.

A few minutes later, the conductor, who was a nice looking blond girl dressed in a red uniform with yellow buttons and white cap, walked toward me and asked for my ticket. I told her that I had left my ticket in my coat pocket with my friends. After a few questions she told me that my train had left the station three minutes before this train and that I would have to purchase another ticket or get off at the next station.

So she stopped the train and I got off at the next station with a pot of water in my hand but without hat or coat, collar or shoes! It was a little station some place in Russia by the name of Lori [?Gori] and I believe the population largely Georgians.

21

I wanted to take a carriage and get to some near city where it would be possible to find a hotel or some place to stay. I hailed a passing carriage whose driver was a woman dressed in a black uniform and wearing a chauffer's cap. She drove two big white horses, so I and the hot water pot went to the city.

The driver went from house to house to find me a place to stay but every place was packed with immigrants. At twelve o'clock when a big town bell rang and the driver turned to me and told me she could do nothing more for me, so I had to get out. She demanded that I pay her fifty rubles. I had kept all my money inside my trousers, so no one would notice that I carried big bills. I objected to giving her the money unless she could find me a place to stay. She called me a "crook" because I did not have a hat or coat. Suddenly she blew lustily on her whistle to call the police. Two officers came running. I was frightened. Since the Turkish deportation and the death of so many of my loved ones, I had feared the police. But the officers acted very kindly. They asked me a few questions and knowing but little Russian, I answered in a broken language. One of the officers smiled at me and asked if I were an Armenian. He told me in Armenian not to be afraid of anything – hearing that, my heart was reassured and I felt very happy and at ease.

The officer conducted us to the Ouchastok police. He told me not to attempt to speak Russian and that he would translate to the Commissioner all that had happened that night. Instead of punishment falling on me, the girl driver was fined and her red tag was taken from her – meaning that she would have to keep her horses in the stable for ten days. I was sorry!

22

When we came out of the station, the new found acquaintance told me he was from Erivan, the capital of Armenia. He asked me to go with him and have a drink. We went a short distance to the corner and down a few steps into a cellar. The candles were burning on a table and a few large barrels were in a corner. The place was packed with girls and men who were drinking and singing. A fat man walked up to us and showed us a table in a corner and we too started drinking. I had never taken so many drinks as I took that night. The constable introduced me to a few of his girlfriends who joined us at our table. Here in this squalor, we stayed until daybreak when this man took me to his own house and gave me a cap and coat. We then started out to look for a place for me to stay. We learned from the hotel keepers that two trains having been held over at this station the night before, all available rooms were taken and that it would be difficult to find a place. However, the news gave me hope that perhaps my friends were here too and that I should be able to find them. I was feeling so ill, not only from the experience of the proceeding night, but from the continuance of the malarial attack and a bad cold, that I could hardly walk around. The constable was very good to me. He took me back to his room and I went to bed while he went out again.

We knew that the people of the town were greatly excited over the Bolsheviks' attacks and rumors were afloat of an uprising. Late in the afternoon, I heard shooting. I could hear women screaming and children crying in the building. When I went out to find how extensive the trouble was, an old lady, in a cotton dress with a shawl around her shoulders, came to me crying and saying, "The Bolsheviks have taken away my son and killed him." In her fear and anguish, she really did not know at the moment what she was doing.

I anxiously waited for the return of my constable friend. I had not heard from him since he had left me in the morning. At last at night, somebody knocked on the door and my doctor friend walked in. He had been told I was there and that I was ill. He knew what to do for me. He gave me some medicine. After a heavy sweat, I felt better and went with him to his hotel to find my other friends, also my hat and coat. I did not see the constable again and do not know to this day whether he was killed in the Bolsheviks' raid or not.

That night after the town had grown quiet we took a train to Poti. This is a small port on the Black Sea. We thought if we could reach this port we might be able to get a small boat and go to Batoum. So, sick as I was, I travelled with my friends for nine tiresome hours in a freight train. This was the only way in which we could reach safety without an investigation by the soldiers.

It was a great moment for the people of that part of Russia, for no one knew whether his neighbor or brother was a radical, or which side they favored. The soldiers also had orders to arrest every foreigner who could not give an exact account of his arrival and facts concerning his identification. Many young boys were being pressed into military service.

When we arrived at Poti, as we could not speak Russian well, and as we did not know the town, we decided to stay in the freight station till daybreak. The place was filled with oily rugs and the accumulated dirt of years.

Our hope now was to reach the piers and watch for a chance of hiring a small boat to take us to Batoum. The political and revolutionary tangles of this part of Russia cannot really be imagined. The Kerensky revolutionary troops were still protecting this part, but just across the border in the Georgian Republic, Armenians and Russians were fighting against the Georgians. All was uncertainty. We could hear, here in Poti, the crash of guns across the border, where the Georgians were fighting the Russians as they did not want the Bolshevik forces to take possession of their land and massacre their people.

23

Late in the evening, we reached the docks and were eagerly scanning the Black Sea with its high waves. Now and again, a glimmer of light showed on the water. Out in the darkness, we suddenly spied a small boat, and seemingly headed toward Batoum. We had been told that no boat from Russia could cross the Black Sea without special permission. We could see a larger ship, a destroyer we thought, probably carrying soldiers to Poti. Evidently the small boat was seen by the man on watch on the larger vessel, for flash! A shell exploded near the little boat. The boat changed its direction and put in at our pier.

It was a motor boat, and already had five passengers for Batoum. These men had rented it, paying almost its actual worth in Kerensky rubles. We learned that the division commander at Poti was a Russian Armenian. The owner of the boat suggested that we go to his headquarters and get permission to have this boat take us to Batoum. This we succeeded in doing. Each of us paid the owner a thousand rubles and, I presume, he in turn paid thousands in graft to get us out from the wharf. So the nine of us in the little boat headed from Batoum.

We thought we could reach Batoum in a day or possibly two. The lights of the city disappeared as we crept out slowly. In the distance we saw the flashlights of the destroyer searching the sea. As we huddled in the boat, we could hear only the roar of the sea and the little boat's motor running. The sea was rough and we could feel the water every moment. The boatman, to avoid the flashlights, headed in the opposite direction from Batoum and out to sea. We were really frightened to put out in such rough weather in so small a craft. But I was worn out and young and in spite of fear, fell asleep hearing the popping of the motor and the boom of the heavy sea.

Early in the morning I awoke. Everything had changed. The sea was quiet, the sun shone brightly and in the distance we could see Batoum, our goal.

We landed at about eleven o'clock. A special guard examined our packages and papers and at last I was actually on my way home. I was glad to be back again and I was glad that I had ten thousand rubles from the trip to give to my mother. As I walked with the doctor, I was teasing him, asking how much money he was taking to his wife. I remember he was angry as I left him and knocked at my mother's door.

My mother exclaimed and warmly greeted me. She saw I was not feeling well and soon had me in bed. I was anxious for the news, for much had happened in such a short time. She told me that my uncle and some of the other young officers had gone to Armenia, where they were organizing volunteer troops to fight against the Turks. She too was planning to return and was only waiting for my arrival.

24

A few weeks passed as we expectantly waited, and finally word came to the Armenian ambassador in Batoum to furnish transportation to the Armenian officers' wives and their families, including the doctor and his family. So, one morning we left Batoum, occupying two freight cars. We were to go to Tiflis first. After two days of slow traveling we reached Tiflis.

We rested that night in the train. Early in the morning I woke up. I was in a valley, and clear sparkling water was running from one side of a mountain. I saw a few small buildings near the railroad track. I saw a sign on one of the buildings in Armenian letters "Gamarlon Station" and I saw a flag, red, blue and orange. I could not believe that this was an Armenian flag and an Armenian station! After a few hours the engine pulled us up the hill to "Black Church" [Karakilise]. I knew this was an Armenian city! I was happy! But I could not express my happiness to anyone. I knew this to be a great climax of my life. At that moment, I could remember all that had happened to us in the last three years. I was thankful to have my mother and uncle with me so we could share the happiness of our lives. I was in my father's country again. I considered everyone I saw at the station a part of my family.

We were all happy when we reached Erivan in the morning. This was the capital city of my dear country. I could not rest all day. I was curious to see everything. My country, my people, my government! I wanted to see the laws enforced by the Armenian government.

I remember I went to the parliament as I had heard several of my teachers from Garin [Erzerum] had been elected to it. I even thought of committing a crime so that I could be punished by an Armenian judge speaking the Armenian language. I knew I was acting foolishly but a great joy was in my heart. My father's country, my country, actually fighting for freedom.

Late in the afternoon I went to bed with another attack of malaria.

25

My uncle, who was in command of a battalion, was ordered to the front. I was fifteen now, and in my mind I looked back on three years and could see him when he was a servant in the Turkish Army. Now he was an officer in his own army fighting against the Turks for the independence of his beloved country. I begged my mother to let me go to the front to watch the Armenian soldiers fight the Turks; the Turks who some years ago massacred a million Armenian Christians. My uncle Garekin, who was the Armenian ambassador to the United States, and who was one of the founders of the Armenian Republic and the Armenian Revolutionary Federation, could use his influence and make it possible for me to go to the front.

Three days later I organized a little group of boys about my age, fourteen or fifteen and, armed with shot guns, we headed for Echmiadzin. This was the holy city of Armenia. The legends say that the baby Christ was brought here and his likeness remained on a cloth in the Church. All the Armenian patriarchs were educated here in the monasteries, and the city was devoted to the Church of Armenia. I was anxious to go to the monasteries and see the old artistic collections that were preserved in a museum there. This is the only town in Armenia that has kept the arts of Armenia from the earliest days, legend says, since long before the days of Christ.

We left Echmiadzin and started for the village of Markara which is located on the Arax River, often called "Mother Arax, the mother of Armenia."

The journey was not long to Markara, a village with a population of about two hundred, the majority of whom are Yezidis. History tells us that this nation or people, once Christian, had embraced the Mohammedan religion. We pressed on and before night reached Igdir. This is near the base of Mount Ararat, our great mountain which rises from the high plateau of Armenia.

I was anxious to reach my uncle. The second battalion of Armenians was positioned to the northwest of Mount Ararat. There are many legends about this area, and I was deeply interested to hear all the stories I could while I was journeying to see my uncle. We reached Mollagmar, the village where the 2nd battalion was stationed, about five o'clock. The population of this village was also made up of Yezidis.

To see the Armenian officers in their gray uniforms and caps and the soldiers in their dark gray uniforms and light gray blouses was indeed interesting to me. This was an Armenian army fighting for freedom! I saw a group of volunteer cavalry climbing the hill. All was absorbing to me.

That night I stayed with my uncle in his tent. We had a long conference. My uncle decided I should go back to Yerivan (Erivan) and take the first train I could to Batoum; from there I was to sail to Constantinople and bring back his mother and sister-in-law. I was more than pleased to accept his suggestion, but before going I wanted to travel in various directions from Mt. Ararat and see some of the places I had known of from my childhood.

This was my land, and I was in it again after three years of wandering among the Turks. I cannot describe how much this meant to me. The snowy summit of Ararat had spoken to the Armenian people for centuries; before the Greeks, before the Romans; this was Armenia!

26

And so we went on horseback, traveling for a number of days, visiting various towns and hearing the legends. We went to Goghp, located in a valley with a hill rising steeply behind it. This hill contains salt mines, and I saw how the industry was carried on by Armenians.

As we were traveling from Goghp to Amia, a little incident happened which revealed much to me about the Armenian character. There were three of us, one an Armenian officer who had lost both of his parents in the Turkish deportations, a boy younger than myself, who had lost all his family, and me. We were talking and singing as we rode along, feeling happy that a little "Armenia" had been returned to us, when we saw two Turks, shepherds, climbing up the mountain. One of us suggested that we might shoot these fellows just for "fun." Revenge was undoubtedly deep in our hearts, but the officer who had suffered much under the Turkish regime advised us not to, saying, "What is the use of killing these innocent men who are really not responsible for the Armenian massacre?" I noticed suddenly that we were all weak hearted, that none of us wanted to kill.

That afternoon we approached a creek we saw not far distant from us the deserted walls of an old Armenian city. This was "Ani" the city that was once the capital of the Kings of Armenia. It is surrounded by a great double wall partly in ruins. The old "patriarchal" church still stands, as does a great palace. This is the city which is traditionally known as "the city of 1001 churches." We only saw three people, two priests and a laborer, living in this deserted place. One of the priests approached us. He was dressed in a black torn robe and had a small greasy fez on his head. I laughed at the first sight of this strange old man. His beard was long, to his waist, and his hair had surely never been cut, but his smile was charming. He was a man who, as we could easily understand, was really sacrificing his life away for mankind in his effort to save the ancient arts of Armenia for the Armenian people. He told us of the life he led, speaking pure Armenian. There were three goats for milking, and old wine, of which he let us drink. The wine was more than fifty years old, for the old man had been there more than half a century. Once he had been a shepherd, but all his people had been massacred during the Sultan Hamid's regime.

We rested here and wandered among the old ruins. Many of the walls were covered with interesting and intricate work. This told us something of the antiquity of our race. Now I know that this is a spot worthy of explorations, research and study – that here the history of the Armenians has been in the making for thousands of years. This was the battleground of many encounters during the early days of Christianity and on down through the middle ages. Then I only knew it was a place held in reverence by our church men and the learned Armenians.

Soon we pressed on to Erivan where my mother was waiting for me.

27

My mother was not surprised when she saw me. She had known that I would be back soon; that my restlessness would not let me stay for many hours in one place. Now I was eager to go to Constantinople as my uncle had planned, but my mother did not want me to go. A few days later we learned that a young man was going from Erivan, so she finally agreed to let me go with him.

Preparations were begun for the journey. Armenian officers who had families in Constantinople gave me money to take with me to their families, as well as letters to various people. I knew that I had uncles there who were wealthy exporters. I also knew that Constantinople was a Europeanized city and that I must buy new clothes so that I would look decent as I walked on the streets. I had with me about twenty rubles when I left the city of Erivan. An Armenian train took us to Tiflis where we changed trains, and the next day we were in Batoum again.

I wanted to obtain a passport from the British Government officials to enter Constantinople, but this would take much red tape and time. I was sitting in a coffee house thinking and wondering, my eyes idly watching others sitting there when a face held my attention. I knew this man but could not place him. He too was looking at me. I suddenly exclaimed "Ardeshes!" I had seen this young man frequently in Garin (Erzeroum) when I was a child. During the war he had been in Constantinople and was now engaged in bringing merchandise from Constantinople to Batoum. We talked over my difficulties; he too was going to Constantinople. He was sure he could land at Trebizon when the ship docked there and get a visa for me as his brother from a Turkish visa officer for a few dollars graft. So that was agreed upon.

Shortly a ship was ready to leave. A young man, a friend of my family, came to me with a small empty suitcase and told me to put my things in it and take it to Constantinople. Several times I was on the point of discarding this bag, but something stayed my hand. At last we were on our way.

Great was our surprise when we found the ship was not to stop at Trebizon. I did not now know what I was to do when I reached Constantinople. For two days we sailed on the Black Sea, and then came to the Bosphorus. It took three hours for the big ship to go through this strait, wriggling into many corners. We could see many beautiful buildings on either side. In the distance we saw a palace, the Sultan's residence. The ship dropped anchor when we were opposite it. Several hours later a small yacht with three flags – British, French and Italian – came to our ship. This was the time I feared, as I had no passport. The officers on the yacht called on the captain, examined the records and discharged all of us. We were now free.

I wanted to go to a hotel, so I could "dress up" and then find my relatives in the morning. I was fifteen, still a boy in years, but a man of many bitter experiences. Responsibility was mine, not to my relatives alone, but to the friends who had entrusted much to me. Now I was in the city of which I had heard so much since I was a small child. I found a room at a hotel, and all that night I dreamed many different things. I could not see the Constantinople of "now" for all the stories I had heard of when I was a little boy. I was in Yerevan again and my father was telling me of this city; stories came back that I could not have recalled during the three tumultuous years that had just passed.

In the morning, after a night of little sleep, I arose and dressed. I wore short blue pants, a black shirt, a Russian hat, brown shoes and long socks. I had bought a nice cane so I would look presentable. I went out and walked on the street called "Pera." This was considered one of the best streets in Constantinople. I noticed all kinds of people passing dressed in many different types of costume. There were only a few European people dressed in beautiful suits. I stopped in a little coffee shop and drank tea. I was nervous, so nervous that I hardly knew what I was doing. I wanted to see my relatives, and yet I hesitated.

Finally, calling a carriage, I asked the driver how long it would take me to go to "Pangalti." He told me it would take two hours, but for five liras he would try to get me there in a shorter time. So taking my suit case we started. In less than an hour and a half we came to my aunt's home. I remembered her from 1913 when she had visited Garin (Erzeroum) but I had never seen my uncle. Therefore I was anxious to visit my aunt first.

A door opened and a nice looking blond girl with glasses came out. She was dressed in a white skirt and red coat. She smiled at me and went back to the door. I inquired from her about my aunt. She exclaimed "Grandmother!" I knew now what I had already felt, that she was my cousin. I should judge she was about sixteen or seventeen. She invited me into the parlor.

As she opened the door for me, just opposite me on the wall hung three pictures, most natural paintings; one was my father, one my old grandmother whom we had lost in the deportation, and one my grandfather whom I had never seen before. This was the first time I had seen a picture of my father since his death. I hesitated going into the room although the pleasant girl was insisting that I sit down and wait a few minutes. She did not know who I was but she was smiling all the time.

Suddenly I felt darkness in my eyes and I fell onto a chair. I did not know just what happened, but when I woke up someone was rubbing my hands and others were crying and sympathizing with me. I am not able to describe a picture of that day. Deep emotions stirred me, my head ached and throbbed; all day visitors came to see me. Word that I had arrived from Armenia had spread rapidly among relatives and friends.

About six o'clock two men came who asked if I had brought a suitcase from Batoum. When I gave it to them, I was very surprised to see them rip through the cover and take out fifty thousand rubles.

I was excited all night.

28

The next day I found my grandmother and aunt whom I was to take back with me. They wanted me to get everything ready so they could leave in a very short time. My poor aunt, whom I remembered as a beautiful girl when she was married to my uncle so few years ago, I could hardly recognize now. She had been forced to marry a Turk during the deportation and had been given to four others. She had brothers in

Constantinople, but she wanted to be away from them. She wanted to forget!

My cousin who had met me on the boat took me to my uncles' house. One whom I remembered from my childhood I wanted to see first. When we entered his house, I noticed sadness among the members of his family. Then I learned that he too was killed. He had been forced to enter Turkish military service.

The family insisted that I stay with them until the cousins, who were young men, returned from their store. When I entered my uncle's bedroom I looked at the pictures on the wall. There one held my eyes. It was another picture of my father. He looked very young, and with him was a beautiful bride. I asked my aunt who it was with my father, and she said "Your Mother." Although she said it was my mother, it did not look to me like my mother whom I had left in Armenia. Passing from that picture I saw my father's picture again, and with him my mother who was in Armenia.

She was dressed in a white wedding gown. Now I was puzzled, and asked questions about the different pictures. My aunt did not know that I had never been told of my own mother's death, so she said to me, "Don't you know that this is Nevart, your mother, and the other one is Zabel?" Then she told me a strange story of my father's very early manhood, how he had fallen into a well, and how my grandmother in anxiety and fear had promised if he could be saved she would give him in marriage to an orphan "Nevart" who was from Arabkir. My father came to Constantinople and was married to her. Two years later, when he brought her to Garin, she died, leaving me the only child, six months old.

My mind was in a whirl, I did not know how, but for some reason I wanted to change my plans of going back. Life looked different. But suddenly something came to my mind. I said to myself, "It doesn't make much difference to me whether she is my real mother or not. Never before in my life have I felt happier than now, when I look back and realize my mother Zabel has given me sincere motherly love; one's own mother could not go through more suffering and disaster than she has been through, and not once during those days and months of misery has she shown the least bit of step-motherliness toward me."

I was very proud of her. As I look back now I do not understand it. I do not know to whom credit should be given, perhaps to both of us that we had lived so closely as mother and son without quarrel since the death of my father. She had protected me many times in our years of wandering; she had cared for me indeed as she would have her own children, the brother and sister whom we had left dead at the scene of the massacre three years before. I see now that she clung to me, the only one left of her household.

I returned to my aunt's house. My aunt saw from my expression that something had happened to me. She sensed that the visit to my uncle's had in some way changed my attitude.

29

The following day, Armenians came to see me to caution me about conditions in Armenia. They wanted information and each was eager to learn of Armenians who were returning to Erivan. They also gave me information about happenings in Garin after our deportation. They told me that many of the jewels which we had kept in the Ottoman bank of Garin, when the Turks deported us, had been sold at auction by the Turkish government. The clothing and valuable rugs had also been sold. Gold had been kept by the Commissioner and was being given back to the people who owned it, if claimed.

I decided I would learn more in detail about this. I went to the Ottoman bank and was shown packages broken open from which diamonds and costly apparel had been taken. There was some gold left but I could not estimate its value. The Commissioner tried to sympathize with me when he read me the itemized account concerning the jewels. I said in reply: "There is no use for you to try and sympathize. I have lost forty-seven lives of my own family and near relatives." He said he was sorry for me, being as young as I was, to have passed through all of this. He assured me nothing else would happen from now on. I laughed at him and left the office.

In order for me to receive the money, as I was under legal age, action had to be taken. A trustee was appointed and for fifteen days, at an expense of more than half I received, I worked to regain a small portion of my heritage. Finally, I received one hundred and fifty liras and a few gold pieces, as against the thousands of liras and wealth in jewels which had been deposited in the Ottoman bank.

Fall had come and my aunt wanted me to give up my ideas of returning to Armenia and to stay in Constantinople and go to school. Here the Armenians were not disturbed and there was every opportunity for me to continue my education that had been so rudely stopped at the time of the deportation. But those long years of wandering and sharing great responsibilities, of making money and assisting my mother, had established habits that were hard for me to forget. For a day and night, my aunt and cousins begged me to remain. My love for, and appreciation of, my uncle in Armenia was great too. I had come for his mother and sister-in-law; I had to take them back. So I finally decided to go to Armenia, get my mother's consent and then return to Constantinople and go to school. I planned to go to the Berberian College, my uncles offering to pay the tuition fees.

My blond cousin's school was next to this college. Both were located in Scutari, Constantinople.

30

Passports were obtained for our return to Armenia and the day set.
It was four o'clock in the afternoon of a late fall day when we started on our journey. Our party consisted of my grandmother, an old lady of about sixty, and my aunt, a beautiful young woman, both dressed in black fur coats, and a nephew of my grandmother's who was a chemist from England and who had decided to go to Armenia to work in the mines. This time I was not so anxious to return to Armenia. Some strange feeling filled my mind, and until the last minute, I was ready to change it. But I had to take my family back!

All night the sea was rough, the next morning my mind was still filled with the desire to stay in Constantinople. As we sat eating our breakfasts, I was thinking especially of my blond cousin and her kindness to me. We observed the many passengers; the ship was packed with intelligent Armenians who were anxious to go to Armenia and render their services to their own red, blue and orange flag. They were deeply excited and happy. One of the men was especially happy. He stood on his chair and spoke. He said this was the greatest moment of his life; he called the attention of the people to the fact that they were returning to an Armenia which was free.

Before he finished his speech, we felt something explode under the ship. Someone cried: "A torpedo!" Everyone rushed to the deck. Perhaps I was still thinking deeply, I do not know, but I did not rush with the first. When I reached the deck, I saw that most of the people had their life preservers on and I saw, too, that we were near the city of Zongouldak. The captain was endeavoring to maintain order and to stop the excitement that was overcoming the passengers. My eyes were held on the life boat and I saw the young man who only a few minutes ago was speaking so full of life and hope. He was anxious to get into the boat. Suddenly the little boat overturned and more than forty people were thrown into the water. Many were drowned and among them the "happy Armenian." Soon we were all transferred to another ship and taken to the nearby port, Zongouldak. Here we stayed overnight and in the morning, once more embarked for Batoum.

Two days later we reached Batoum without further incident. My grandmother and aunt were eager to be on our way. As soon as possible, we obtained transportation, and in twenty-four hours, we were in Armenia.

31

When the train stopped at Erivan station, which is some distance from the center of the city, I thought I would run and see my mother. I wanted to see her before the others. I found her in bed, as it was early morning. She was happy and crying for joy when I gave her the news of her mother and sister-in-law. She kissed me but she knew nothing that had changed for me.

Hurriedly she dressed and went to the station with me. Here she greeted her mother and sister, whom she had not seen since the deportation. What must have gone through the minds of these women! So much had happened. Life was utterly changed for everyone. My uncle came back to Erivan on leave, to be with his dear mother.

My young aunt, who had been in the hands of the Turks during the deportation, was ill. She asked me if I could help her go to see a doctor. She did not want my uncle and mother to know. She trusted me and needed help. I can still see her as I saw her then. Still very young, not more than twenty-one, with beautiful long black hair and great brown eyes and, in the old days, always with a charming smile on her face. When I was a little child she played games with me, even though I was five years younger. I knew she liked me and trusted me. I found a doctor and he assured me he could cure her but it would cost a great deal. She did not want my mother or my uncle to know about her illness, but I knew she was a victim of the diseased Turks.

Trouble started again between the Armenians and Turks. They were fighting in the city of Kars. I wanted to get away from the worries and cares. The old illness of malaria had returned and I was physically unfit to face more suffering. I was sixteen now and the thought of college called strongly to me. My mother had given me some money, but in turn, I had given this to my young aunt, so I felt I could not ask for more. My mother had begun to suspect that I was spending my money in bad places. I knew she had great confidence in me. So at last I went to her and made her promise that she would ask me no questions, but I was going to ask for money to go back to Constantinople.

She knew from my manner that I was no longer the same Souren I used to be. I hated everything, even the things in which I was deeply interested. Everything had changed.

During my absence my mother had received a letter telling her to come to Constantinople in order to share some of the money and jewels which had been kept by the Turkish government. So now that she knew I wanted to return, she said she would go also, if I would wait for her. She did not want to leave her mother so abruptly. I knew she loved her mother deeply and her mother clung to her because she was the only daughter who had lived through the wild Turkish massacres.

She would have to leave the little girl whom she believed to be her daughter and yet she decided to go. She begged me to tell her everything I was keeping from her. Her heart was torn with anxiety.

32

She had to leave the little girl whom she believed to be her daughter. Her mother would care for the child while she was gone. Much might be gained for her family by this trip.

My heart was divided. This was not my mother, yet she loved me. My own mother's people were in Constantinople. The city, the opportunity for study, and beyond that, the blond cousin to whom my boy's heart had gone out called me. My mother sensed the difference. She begged me to tell her what was in my heart that was separating us. Finally, we were on our way. The "goodbyes" were said and I was again leaving my beloved Armenia. But this time I was eager to be gone. Sixteen is young in years, but may be old in sorrow; and this was a new sorrow. A disquiet which made life uncertain – the goal was no longer clear and definite. I could be educated and then I would return to serve my people and my land.

And so we traveled again to Batoum, again we crossed from end to end the beautiful Black Sea, and in a few days entered the wonderful city, Constantinople again. We visited all our friends and relations. Many of these my mother had not seen for years. Tears and smiles came quickly; gladness and sorrow were close together during these days.

33

Arrangements were made for me to enter the college at Scutari.

This school was founded by Reteyos Berberian and was considered one of the best Armenian schools. I remember how I felt when my mother paid the fee for the first semester. It was hard for me to continue my education that had been interrupted so badly, to adapt myself again to the routine of school life. But I was anxious to get away from the world and study in order that someday I could take an office in Armenia, my beloved country.

My aunts and mother came frequently to see me. During these days my mother was seeking a way to verify my father's estate and attempting to salvage a remnant of the wealth that might have been ours.

Days passed quickly as I made new acquaintances, but still a cloud hung over me.

Sometime later a telephone message came to me from Constantinople. A cousin was speaking who was employed in the New York Life Insurance Company. He said he had two pieces of good news for me: one was about my aunt who had been married the night before and he said that I had been "best man" at the wedding, and the second news item was that my mother had left the city taking with her the jewels which belonged to my own dead mother and which had been with my father's estate in the bank in Constantinople.

I had only a few cents at the time but I ran from the school in Scutari without permission with only one thought to reach my aunt's house in Constantinople. What had my cousin meant, first that I was "best man", second that my mother had gone! I knew my mother loved me. She would not leave without kissing me "goodbye." Through all the years of suffering she had not deserted me. I knew my relatives in Constantinople did not like my stepmother's side of the family as there had always been too much love for our country among her people. They had been revolutionists and had sought a free Armenia. When I reached my aunt's house, my second cousin, whom I liked more than anyone in the house, greeted me with a smile. I was strangely excited and crying without knowing why. I told her of the telephone message which I had received and she interpreted it.

My aunt Makrig had been married the night before at my uncle's house and his son whose name was also "Souren" had been best man.

She told me a strange story about my mother: one that has changed my life. My mother had discovered that the jewels of my own dead mother and my father's insurance had been left in my name but the jewels had been surrendered to her, as my guardian, as well as some of my father's estate. My relatives in Constantinople were trying to get the jewels from her. That was the reason for her sudden and hasty departure. It wasn't the money part that worried me but my mother's action – what did it mean? Dark depression took possession of me.

My male cousins, kind, friendly young men, came from their city offices. They joked and laughed at me but in a kindly way. They were trying to make me feel happy.

It was much harder now for me to go back to school. No word came from my mother. My deep interest was in my blond cousin, who was also in school at Tbrotsaser College in Scutari. I wanted to be near her in my trouble; this feeling finally won in my troubled soul, and I returned to school.

This time I had a different interest in life. I had heard many times how money and jewels can change a person. So I thought as soon as my mother had an opportunity she had expressed her real self. She had left me without resources in a strange city. She knew that I hated my uncles because I remembered when we were being deported and had lost all we had, money, family, home, we had tried to get help from them and had not even received a letter of sympathy although there were ways by which they could have communicated. I did not in any way want to be obligated to them.

34

The afternoon of my return to school stands as a picture in my mind. The principal of the school was the son of the late Reteos Berberian, the founder, who was a poet. An assembly was being held and recitations were part of the program. My own particular part was the recitation of beautiful poems, a favorite of the principal's father. It was a dramatic scene depicting a young soldier in love with a princess and the obstacles that surrounded them. The principal wanted it performed with dramatic expression and he had chosen me for this. Suddenly, I heard my name called but I refused, because I knew I could not do justice to the beautiful legend with my own mind in such turmoil. I was told to report to the office after school. Here in the office I met with understanding sympathy. Mr. Berberian told me I did not need to accept the assistance of anyone; that at some future time I would be able to repay him and that he intended to keep me in the school.

So the weeks went by, I studied hard and the quiet regular life helped me. Only the fact that no word came to me from my mother or relatives, other than my own mother's sister, weighed on my heart.

Christmas holidays were nearing. Everyone in the school was planning his vacation. I only wanted to see my aunt and be with her for a few days in Constantinople.

A week before the school closed I received a letter from Paris. Since coming to Constantinople I had learned that my dead mother's own brother was in Paris, that he was a man of independent means and was highly educated. It was indeed a surprise to me to learn that he had heard of my situation in Paris and now he wrote offering me a home and an education. He assured me in his letter that he would do everything for my happiness.

I could not think of taking this step without consulting my aunt. My heart was bitter toward my uncles in Constantinople whom I knew wanted me to leave that part of the world so that no one would know that I was in need of money.

35

But vacation came – a happy vacation and my heart sang as a boy's heart will sing when love enters in. My blond cousin was having her vacation too and together we danced and played and made merry. I look back and see those days as being shining and luminous; perhaps more so, because of the contrast with anxiety and sorrow which had been mine. We met and planned, planned a future as all youth does; of the time when we should be together. We often had our trysting place under a statue of the Turkish Constitution Hurriyet Tepesi.

At last the short vacation was over, but life was different now. My cousin was not far away and letters made the hours fly quickly.

36

The months passed quickly and summer had almost come, when my aunt's son returned to Constantinople from Cilicia, where he had been serving as a volunteer in the French-Armenian Legion. His coming was to bring about a great change in my life, of which I was totally unaware. At this same time, I was endeavoring to have my father's insurance, which named me beneficiary, made over to me. I knew if I could succeed in this, I should be able to stay in the school during the summer months and complete the course.

We were preparing for examinations. In the classroom I was assisting other students in mathematics. One day, as we were working over a difficult problem, a messenger appeared and gave me a letter from the Life Insurance Company. It stated that I was to be at the Company's office at two o'clock to receive my check for 1,600 English Liras [Pounds Sterling]. At first I thought this was a joke. I dropped my mathematics and began figuring on the account I would receive.

Without getting permission, I hurried from the school and went to the office to receive the check. Everything was ready for me there and in a few minutes the check was in my hands and I was again on my way.

I was child enough to show off to my uncles, but I was especially glad that they had not helped me and that I was not indebted to them.

I paid my debts at the school and bought new suits and shoes for the school's closing exercises.

On the day of closing, I received two letters from my uncles in Constantinople inviting me to spend my vacation at their homes. I laughed. This year had taught me some strange and interesting insights into human nature.

The Berberian College final exercises were held in a Memorial Hall built in honor of the great Raffi, who was an outstanding Armenian writer and whose memory was revered by all Armenians. Dr. Berberian, the principal, knew this was a happy day for me and once again I was encouraged to recite his father's favorite poem. He knew I would not fail him this time. The hall was crowded, my cousins, uncles and my one dear aunt were all there and when my position of second in the class was announced, there was great applause.

When the assemblage was dismissed, I judged my uncles were waiting for me, but I went out and went with my aunt. I knew that she really loved me.

37

Summer passed. My cousin who was back from the war in Cilicia was restless. He made all his plans and announced to the family that as soon as he could get his American visa he was going for a trip to America. This was the first time "America" had come close to me. I told him I would go with him if he would wait until I could get my passport. It took about ten days as a rule. I hurried down town at about eleven in the morning and by three in the afternoon had all my papers ready.

Now we were going to America! Our interest was great during those days. We studied our geographies and histories, every detail was interesting. We understood that America had a democratic government and that the laws were made by the people's representatives, that there was no religious persecution, that it was a free country.

Many of our friends and relatives tried to discourage us from going to a country which would make us forget our native land. I now realize that was the impression my friends had about America. So in 1921, when I was eighteen years old, I sailed for America.

Epilogue

I have long since been an American citizen and as I hear Americans speak of the backgrounds of the naturalized citizen and ask "What of culture?", "What of ideals?", "Can the foreign-born understand our ideals, freedom, equality, justice and equal opportunity before the law?" I answer in my soul: "Can you appreciate freedom until a price has been set upon your head and you have wandered, a hunted being, for years?" "Can you cherish a law that holds all men equal, until you have, many times, because there was little justice for a Christian, passed almost into the valley of death?"

FAMILY TREE

HANNESIAN MARTAYA

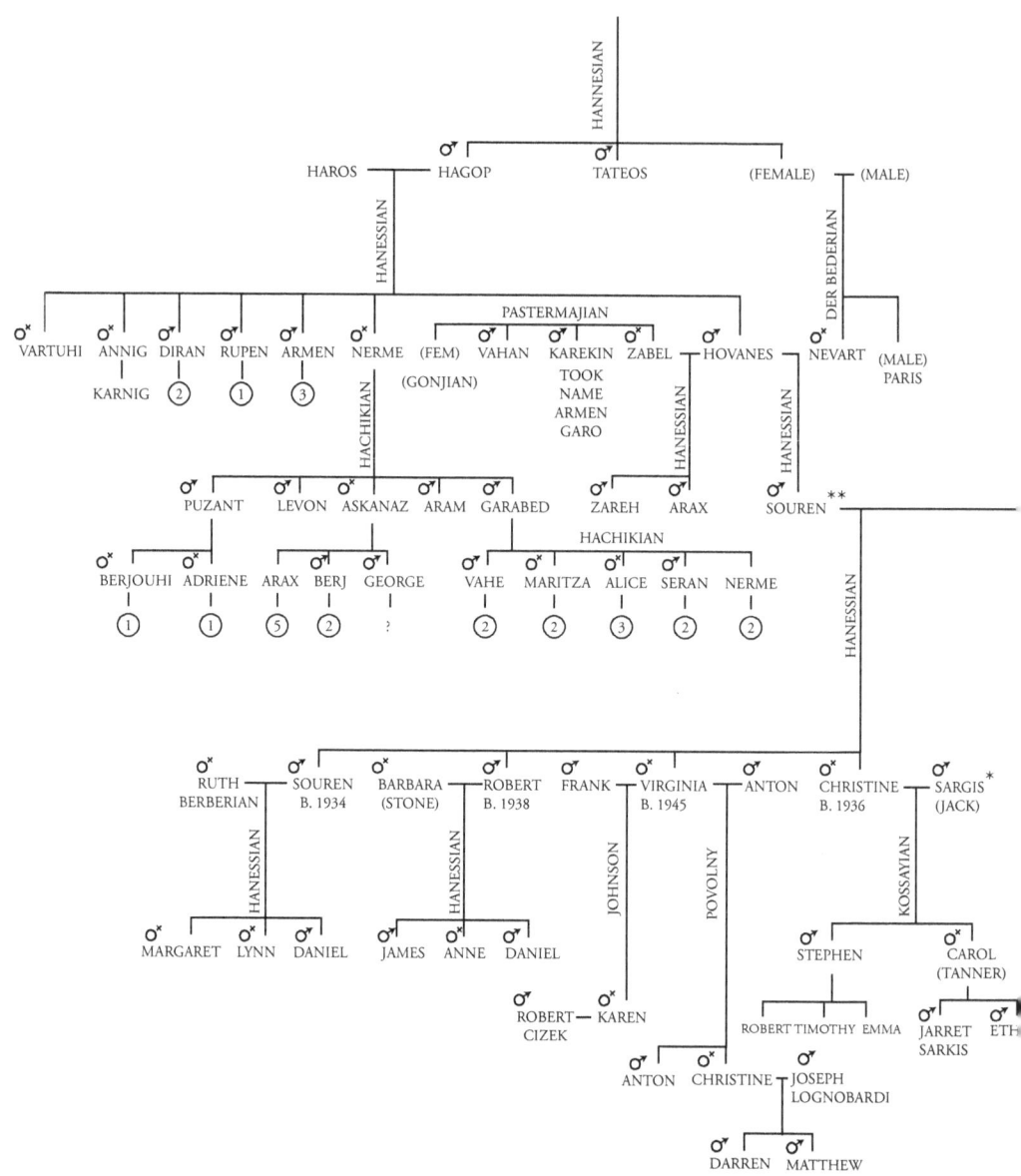

KARAGUZIAN FAMILY TREE

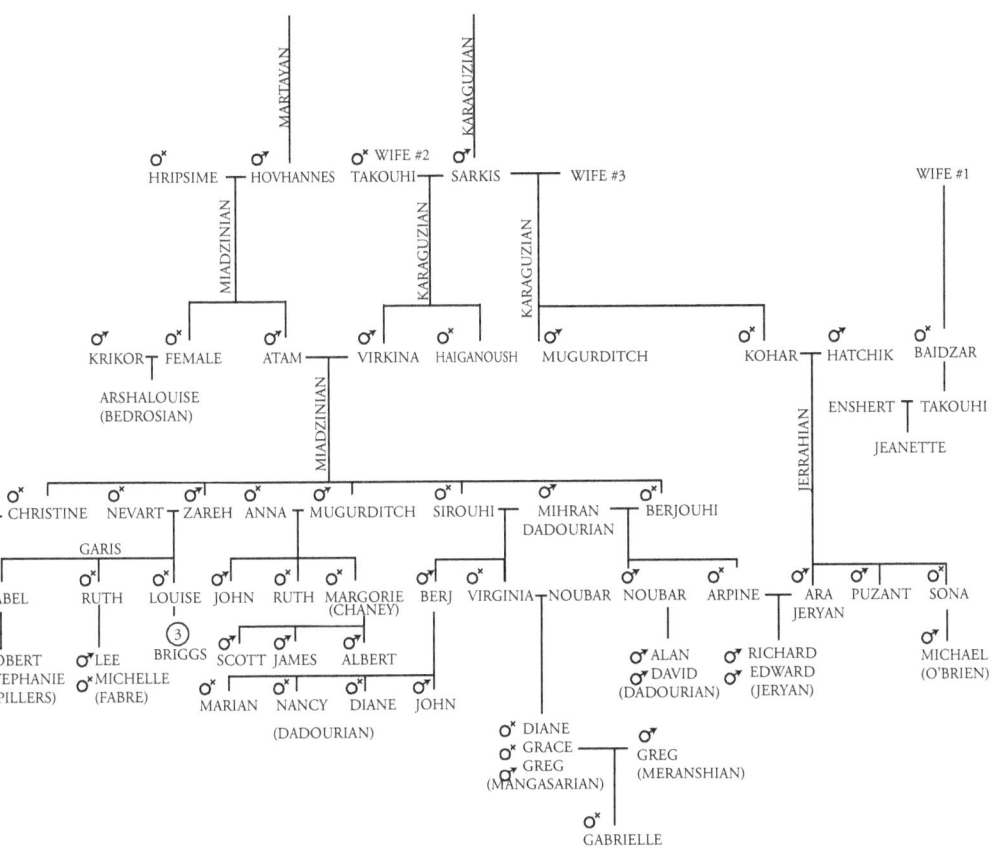

* Drew up this family tree in 1980
** Author of this book

GOMIDAS INSTITUTE

The Gomidas Institute is an independent academic institution dedicated to modern Armenian studies and research.

Gomidas Institute, 42 Blythe Rd., London W14 0HA, England.
www.gomidas.org

Gomidas Institute Books on Armenian Genocide

Hagop K. Beshlian, *A Shirt for the Brave*, 2017.

Gretchen Rasch, *The Storm of Life: A Missionary Marriage from Armenia to Appalachia*, 2016.

Henry Morgenthau, *Ambassador Morgenthau's Story*, 2016.

Papken Injarabian, *Azo the Slave Boy and his Road to Freedom*, transl. from French by Elisabeth Eaker, 2015.

Jean V. Gureghian, *My Father's Destiny: The Golgotha of Armenia Minor*, transl. from French by Diran Meghreblian with a preface by Yves Ternon, 2015.

Avedis Albert Abrahamian, *Avedis' Story: An Armenian Boy's Journey*, ed. with an intro. by Carolann Najarian, 2014.

Lewis Einstein, *Inside Constantinople: A Diplomatist's Diary During the Dardanelles Expedition, April-September, 1915*, 2014.

Thomas K. Mugreditchian, *The Diyarbekir Massacres and Kurdish Atrocities*, with an intro. by Ugur Üngör, 2013.

Anne Elizabeth Elbrecht, *Telling the Story: The Armenian Genocide in the Pages of The New York Times and Missionary Herald*, (with an intro. by Dikran Kouymjian), 2012.

Ara Sarafian (comp., ed. and intro.), *Talaat Pasha's Report on the Armenian Genocide*, 2011.

Ara Sarafian (comp., ed. and intro.), *United States Official Records on the Armenian Genocide 1915-1917*, 2004.

Henry Morgenthau, *United States Diplomacy on the Bosphorus: The Diaries of Ambassador Morgenthau, 1913-1916*, 2004.

James Bryce and Arnold Toynbee, *The Treatment of Armenians in the Ottoman Empire, 1915-16: Documents Presented to Viscount Grey of Fallodon by Viscount Bryce [Uncensored Edition]*, edited and with an introduction by Ara Sarafian, 2005, 2nd ed.

James L. Barton (comp.), *Turkish Atrocities - Statements of American Missionaries on the Treatment of Armenians in Ottoman Turkey 1915-1917*, 1998.

Maria Jacobsen, *Diaries of a Danish Missionary: Harpoot, 1907-1919*, 2006.

Tacy Atkinson, *The German, the Turk and the Devil Made an Alliance: Harpoot Diaries, 1909-1917*, 2016 [second printing].

Yervant Odian, *Accursed Years: My Exile and Return from Der Zor, 1914-1919*, transl. from original Armenian by Ara Stepan Melkonian with an intro. by Krikor Beledian, 2009.

Aram Andonian, *Exile, Trauma and Death: On the Road to Chankiri with Komitas Vartabed*, transl., ed. and annot. by Rita Soulahian Kuyumjian, 2012.

Paul Leverkuehn, *A German Officer during the Armenian Genocide: A Biography of Max von Scheubner-Richter*, transl. from German by Alasdair Lean with a preface by Jorge Vartparonian and a historical introduction by Hilmar Kaiser, 2009.

Abram I. Elkus, *The Memoirs of Abram Elkus: Lawyer, Ambassador, Statesman*, with a commentary by Hilmar Kaiser, 2004.

Varteres Mikael Garougian, *Destiny of the Dzidzernag: Autobiography of Varteres Mikael Garougian*, transl. from the Armenian manuscript by Mariam V. Sahakian, 2005.

Ruth Parmelee, *Pioneer in the Euphrates Valley*, 2002.

George Horton, *Blight of Asia*, with a foreword by James W. Gerard and a new intro. by James L. Marketos 2nd ed., London: Sterndale Classics, 2008.

Rafael de Nogales, *Four Years beneath the Crescent*, transl. from Spanish by Muna Lee, London: Sterndale Classics, 2003.

Harry Stuermer, *Two War Years in Constantinople: Sketches of German and Young Turkish Ethics and Politics* [revised and complete edition], with a critical introduction to new edition by Hilmar Kaiser, London: Sterndale Classics, 2004.

Grace Knapp, *The Tragedy of Bitlis*, London: Sterndale Classics, 2002.

Clarence Ussher, *An American Physician in Turkey*, London: Sterndale Classics, 2002.

Note: Sterndale Classics is an imprint of the Gomidas Institute.